Praise for
Remembering Who You Are

"Ms. Shinn has written a spiritual gem. If you are in a place of vague discomfort, or merely working out the details of your own spiritual growth, you will benefit from her experience, authenticity, and insights. This book should be on your bedside table."

-- **Terry Pearce**, founder of Leadership Communication, UC Berkeley adjunct professor (retired), and author of *Lead Out Loud* and *Clicks and Mortar*

"Remembering Who You Are is a fresh, clear light illuminating the path of spiritual growth. Its wisdom makes the journey clear. Its deep understanding feels like the gentle, wise hand of a learned friend supporting us on the most meaningful journey of our lives."

-- **Reverend David McArthur,** senior minister Unity of Walnut Creek, and author of *The Intelligent Heart*

"In clear, concise language, Shinn explores the essentials of metaphysical awakening. She has a unique ability to take a complex subject and make it not only accessible, but illuminating. Remembering Who You Are is a book for beginners and advanced seekers alike."

-- **Z Egloff**, author of *Verge*

"Remembering Who You Are is a powerful book that sends a gentle invitation to its readers to listen internally for what life intends for you. It is exciting to be on this journey and to recognize that rather than following superficial pursuits and outside heroes, you can look in the mirror and find your own true hero. Inspiring and thought-provoking!"

-- **Jessica Doigny**, LCSW, hospice bereavement coordinator

"In Remembering Who You Are, the author's voice comes through as one of humility, experience, and expertise, providing a plethora of information that will move you ahead in your ascension process whether you consider yourself a novice or one of the well informed. I will definitely keep this book handy as a reference for my energy work."

-- **Kate Gorman**, minister, Reiki master, special education instructor, and human services counselor

Remembering Who You Are

A Guide to Spiritual Awakening and Inner Peace

JILL SHINN

A *Wake Up, Sweetheart* Publication

Dedication

For my husband, John, and my beautiful children, Julia and Jordan, who are constant sources of inspiration to me. Thank you for your love, support, and wisdom, and thank you for choosing to be with me in this lifetime. I adore you.

And for my parents, Sylvia and Robert Vanasek, who provided just the right *stuff* to set me on my path. Mom, thank you for always honoring my space and privacy, and Dad, thank you for your warmth and sense of humor. I love you both.

Contents

Acknowledgments

I would like to thank everyone who supported me throughout the writing of this book, as well as everyone who has played a role in my spiritual development.

To my draft readers: Kate Gorman, Z Egloff, Vicki McCaslin, Jessica Doigny, Scott Shnurman, Linda Camezon, John Shinn, Jen Pearce, and David Hirata. Your feedback was pure gold.

To my lightworker posse and meditation group, fearlessly led by Cecilia Ampon. Words cannot adequately express the love and growth I've experienced with all of you.

To my dear friends at Unity of Walnut Creek. Your affection and confidence in me are so very much appreciated. Thank you Reverend David McArthur for your support and encouragement.

To Z Egloff and Natalie Purcell, for traveling this path before me and demonstrating that it can be done.

To Jeff McCaslin for his guidance in the art direction of this book.

To Terry Pearce for his wisdom and generosity.

To my extended family, including the Vanaseks, the Emanuels, the Palmers, the Svedbergs, the Strybles, the Whitneys, the Ponomareffs, the Weirs, and the (ever expanding) Shinns.

To my sister and friend, Dawn, my brother, Bill, and their families.

To my parents, Bob and Sylvia. Thank you for your constant love and support.

To my husband, John, and my children, Jordan and Julia. You are my sweethearts.

To my teachers and most inspiring role models: Deepak Chopra, Marianne Williamson, Eckhart Tolle, Abraham, Shakti Gawain, Steve Rother, Doreen Virtue, Julia Cameron, Louise Hay, Thich Nhat Hahn, Elizabeth Gilbert, Jane Austen, Carl Jung, Joseph Campbell, and Dr. Seuss!

To all of my angels and spirit helpers. I can feel you with me, illuminating my path, one step at a time. Thank you, God!

Introduction

This is a book about spiritual awakening and transformation, and if you've been guided to read it, it means that you, along with millions of other people, have already begun the awakening process. You may even be further along the path than you realize.

To "wake up" implies that we have been asleep spiritually, which is the typical result of being born into a dualistic world where we humans must develop an ego—an independent, *separated* identity—just to graduate from kindergarten.

So most of us did just that. We came here, developed an ego, and proceeded as if this was who we truly were until one day who we always *thought* we were wasn't enough anymore. The money didn't make us happy. Having children didn't fulfill us. The prince on a white horse turned out to be an ordinary guy driving his mom's old station wagon. Or perhaps a devastating crisis caused us to reevaluate absolutely everything.

Before sharing my personal story of awakening, let me tell you about someone I know. This story represents a typical, nondramatic example of the early stages of spiritual awakening and provides a quick overview of the premise of this book.

Two years ago I mentioned to a friend that I was planning to write a book on spiritual awakening. She asked me what that meant, and I told her that I believed we were all primarily spiritual beings who came to earth for the purpose of learning certain lessons. These lessons could only be learned by living in physical bodies, being partially separated from our higher spiritual selves, and forgetting the essence of who we are, which is God. Spiritual awakening, therefore, is the process of remembering and reclaiming our true spiritual identity and anchoring that in on a deep level.

I explained that each of us *volunteered* to come here, which required us to increase the density of our energy bodies and be born into physical bodies, lifetime after lifetime. We did this not only for our own growth and expansion, but for the growth and expansion of the entire universe. We knew that lessons learned in the *trenches* of physical reality would be the most permanent and profound, and yet not every being in the universe would be cut out for the extreme challenges of earthly life.

When a soul in a physical body learns to experience the truth of his divinity while surrounded by illusions of separation and death, he accomplishes perhaps the greatest spiritual feat possible. For this, we humans are honored throughout the universe, not only for our heroic courage and perseverance, but for our willingness to serve as leaders and guides to other souls.

I went on to tell my friend that these lessons and this process of transformation are what we came here to experience, and that I would share information and insights that would assist my readers in their own individual processes.

My friend stared at me for a moment and then said, "Honestly, this all sounds like a lot of work, and if I am happy with my life just the way it is, *which I am*, why would I want to stir everything up?"

I was a bit surprised at this response because it had always been my personal nature to plumb the depths of mind and soul for answers to what I felt were life's most pressing questions: Who are we? Where did we come from? Why are we here? After a moment, I conceded, "Well, if you're happy, then you must be where you need to be, because joy and fulfillment are signs that you're on the right path."

Ten months later, at a party, I overheard my friend engaged in a conversation with a mutual friend, a physician. She said, "...I just don't know if my career in sales is still right for me. I enjoy my work, and I'm good at it, but I don't feel like I'm really *doing* anything. I mean, you're a doctor who helps people physically, and Jill helps people spiritually, but all I'm doing is selling products. It just doesn't seem like enough anymore." I looked at her face and saw that she was *now* struggling. The contentment she had expressed in our prior conversation had given way to doubts and confusion.

At first I wondered if I had planted these seeds of discontent, but then I realized that regardless of how the shift had occurred, my friend had begun her own process of awakening, and that was something to be celebrated. This is not to say that being spiritually *conscious* is necessarily better than being happily immersed in our worldly existence (after all, joy is joy, and that's our divine nature whether we're keenly aware of our spiritual identity or not), but if we came here to expand our consciousness and to wake up to our highest possible good, then it is a happy moment when a friend opens her eyes, stretches, and says, "Wow, I had the most amazing dream. We were all there together, in this beautiful garden with luminescent flowers, and we could *fly*…!"

Of course, the initial stages of spiritual awakening don't always feel magical. They can be disorienting and disruptive. In fact, what we refer to as a "wake up call" can be excruciating. We've all had them to some degree or another: accidents, brushes with death, devastating relationship break-ups, health scares, losses of loved ones, horrifying nightmares, etc.

When we're spinning our wheels and not going anywhere, when our priorities are jumbled, or when we're doing damage to ourselves or others, we may get hit with a *cosmic two-by-four*. If you disregard the gentle, loving voice of spirit, it will get louder and louder until you can't ignore it. Enter the wake-up call.

The good news is that most consciously aware people eventually recognize the value of the cancer, or the job loss, or the divorce, because it shook them up enough to reexamine where they were going, which was slightly, or perhaps more that slightly, off course. It got them to open their eyes and get back on track spiritually, which is why we are all here, whether we realize it or not.

The seeds of my personal story of spiritual awakening were planted about the time I flunked my first year of kindergarten. It seems I was naturally resistant to forming a good, solid ego, because there I stood watching my graduating classmates march proudly forward into first grade without me.

Even though I was only five years old, the message was clear: This earth thing was *not* going to be easy. Whatever I was doing wasn't good enough, and I'd have to work harder, be friendlier, get with the program. But in the back of my mind, I vaguely remembered a time and place where I was everything I needed to be and no one would have suggested anything different.

As I grew up, I continued feeling homesick for something I didn't remember. I did my work, had supportive-enough friends and family, and spent a lot of time in my room journaling and reading books like, *Man's Search for Meaning* by Victor Frankl, and *Illusions* by Richard Bach. I was different—didn't feel like I fit in. I searched outside for answers to life's questions, and I searched inside for ways that I could feel better, *be* better somehow.

College was perhaps the lowest point. One Saturday I found myself wandering around the huge campus looking for someone, *anyone*, I knew. I was lost, metaphorically, and I cried out to the universe to show me the way. I had taken a series of wrong turns, but I knew that some sort of higher power existed that could help me get back on track.

What happened next was remarkable. Over the next few days, I had three astonishing psychic experiences that were largely foreign to me, as I had never experienced that sort of thing before. In each situation I had a crystal-clear premonition about something that was about to happen, and those events occurred *exactly* as I had foreseen them. The third time was a charm because I realized in no uncertain terms that I was being shown that everything is connected. We are all interrelated, and we have spiritual helpers to assist us if we will only ask.

After that, things took an upward turn. I graduated from college, got a great job, bought a brand new car, and found a nice boyfriend. But within a couple years, the physical world's version of success was not enough for me, and I started searching again. I meditated, went for psychic readings, saw various therapists, read stacks of books, did bodywork, breath work, attended endless spiritual and self-help workshops, learned about angels and spirit guides, and studied various spiritual systems. I just took it all in, kept what worked for me, and threw out the rest.

About the same time, I went to graduate school and eventually became a psychotherapist. But before long, I became dissatisfied with the many limitations of psychotherapy and left my private practice. It was clear to me that more concrete progress was made when we bypassed the ego than when we engaged it by exploring our problems week after week.

As a result of this, I became interested in energy work and intuitive work and received training in Reiki healing, angel-related therapy, and other modalities. Ultimately I found that everything I had ever learned or experienced, every success and every failure, was needed to propel me along the path of spiritual awakening, as is true for everyone.

I became a spiritual counselor, teacher, and writer, and while I can't claim to be a fully enlightened human being, I

have seen myself and many others become positively transformed by tapping into the power of spirit. It is now my highest purpose and honor to help and guide fellow travelers on
their spiritual journeys.

In the following pages, I will integrate and present some
the best and most valuable information and insights available
to aid you in progressing on your uniquely individual path
of spiritual awakening and ascension. I say *individual* because
there is no one magic formula, no universal right way. This
guide is specifically designed to help you find your own special path, your own *inner* guidance, and follow it to your highest good.

The word "Yoga" means *union*, and the purpose of the yogic traditions and practices is to find union of body and mind,
union of self and God, union of individual and others. How
you achieve this may be through meditation, formal religion,
service, scholarly pursuits, the arts, etc. *Your* Yoga is your own
personal way of getting closer to God, and ultimately only
you can decide what that way will be.

In addition to helping you find your own path, the ideas
and information in these pages are presented for the purpose
of jogging your memory, helping you truly *remember who you
are*. Keep what works for you, and disregard the rest.

Part 1 explains more about the awakening and ascension
processes and why *now* is a critical period in the evolution of
humanity. Here we will explore our spiritual roots, as well as
look at and compare some of the most highly effective paths
leading to enlightenment.

Part 2 is entitled "Remembering Spiritual Law." This section provides an overview of the most relevant universal laws

operating in our world, laws that dictate whether we humans make slow or rapid progress on our spiritual paths. We will all get there eventually, but understanding and accepting the "game rules" can accelerate the process and make life a lot more pleasant.

Part 3 helps you get clear about who you are as a human being and then shows you how to accelerate the process of releasing everything that no longer serves you, as well as taking actions that raise your spiritual vibration. You will learn various simple but potent practices and techniques that will help you step into and remember your full spiritual power.

I recommend that you read this book from beginning to end without skipping around, as earlier sections build a foundation for those that follow. Also, as you read I encourage you to make a habit of checking in with your internal guidance. Some material will feel like a perfect fit for you, while other material may not. That's okay. Ask yourself, "Does this feel true to me?" The answer may be yes, and it may be no. Always honor that.

If however you find yourself strongly resisting or reacting to something, anything, it would serve you to take a look at where this is coming from. That goes for anything you actively reject in your life. There's a big difference between not believing something and having an emotional *reaction* to something you don't believe. When this happens, give yourself a gift, and ask your guidance to help you understand the basis of the reaction. These moments will serve your path every bit as much as the moments when you feel peacefully at one with yourself, the universe, and this book.

Enjoy this journey, and know that the universe supports you, and so do I.

PART I

Your Personal
Evolution

ONE

Awakening to Spirit

What is spiritual awakening, and what does it mean to remember who we are? As pure spiritual beings, we possess clarity and perspective, but as mortals, we are challenged by human minds that are subject to fear and distortion, minds that can lead us to great suffering. The good news is that it is possible for our minds to undergo a great *transformation* of consciousness while still in the physical body. This can occur spontaneously or result from meditation and focused intention. Either way, it always involves divine grace.

This transformation goes by many names. In the Hindu tradition, it is called *enlightenment*. In Buddhism, it is called *the end of suffering* or sometimes enlightenment. In the Christian religion, it is *salvation,* and in New Age or New Thought circles, it is called *awakening* or the process of *ascension* (which has other connotations that will be discussed later).

As humans, we are born with two qualities of being. We possess an individual identity or *lower self*, which is made up of physical and energetic bodies, including an ego and personality. This is a temporary self, created for the purpose of having a 3-D mortal experience.

Above and beyond this local self, we have a *Higher Self* that is, always has been, and always will be connected with source energy, or God. At our core, each of us is a spark of divine source energy, and nothing we can do as human beings can change our fundamental spiritual nature.

The ego state that most people live in is based on the limitations of existential life. Like the brain, the ego is a constrictor. We were given an ego to direct our attention to this particular time, space, and incarnation. Spirit lives a timeless, infinite existence, but that is not what we came *here* for. We came into these bodies for a focused and physically based experience. We came here to express ourselves uniquely as one aspect of God. We came here to lose our way and then find it again, in even a grander sense.

Being Present

For the most part, the lower self remains unconscious of the Higher Self until we begin the awakening process, when the *thinking* and compulsive *doing* of the ego give way to the beautiful *being* state of spirit. This can happen suddenly, but it usually occurs gradually over time, and once this process has begun, it cannot be reversed. It can only be impeded by the ego, whose survival may feel threatened.

Spiritual teacher Eckhart Tolle writes, "Awakening is a shift in consciousness in which thinking and awareness separate...Instead of being in charge of your life, thinking becomes the servant of awareness. Awareness is conscious connection with universal intelligence."[1]

Awareness, mindfulness, and *presence* all describe the simple function of *being.* "Beingness" is our natural, God-given state, and there is no thinking or judging involved. It is consciousness without thought, and the inner purpose we all share is to remember and regain this awakened state of being.

When you notice yourself stopping everything to enjoy a simple, everyday moment, you have had a glimpse of awareness. Once you have had this conscious experience, you can choose to have it again. In fact, the more you practice being present, the easier it gets. You begin to realize that the special moments in life are independent of special occasions or circumstances. You really cannot plan for them because they happen spontaneously, outside of your control. In fact, sometimes planning for "a good time" can just set you up for disappointment.

On the other hand, when you're present in the moment, the most mundane situations can take on an unexpectedly magical quality—like when a child captivates you with a story or when a stranger does something so kind you feel your heart expand. When you're busy planning tomorrow, you don't even notice these moments, but when you're in that pure state of being, these become some of your most treasured memories, and you recognize "strangers" as your brothers and sisters. That is the meaning of awareness.

Awakening can also be described as a shift in authority from the ego to the Higher Self. Either way, this shift occurs spontaneously when one is ready on a deep level to take the next step in her spiritual evolution, and not before. Although the ego might enjoy perceiving itself as "enlightened," it cannot bring about this shift through effort or will. Ironically, the ego can only contribute to the awakening process by learning to take a back seat to the Higher Self.

So what does it look like when someone begins to awaken? This varies from person to person. For some it is a subtle, and for others dramatic. For some it is sudden, and for others it spans a lifetime. Sometimes it's fun and exciting, and other times painful and disturbing. For some it involves flashing lights and angelic visitations, while for others it is preceded by feelings of hopelessness. It might begin with a sense that what was previously satisfying no longer is or, conversely, that what was previously dull now takes on a certain glow. Often there's a feeling of being between worlds, because we are no longer driven by the ego's desires, but are not yet integrated spiritually.

What Is Ascension?

Visionary Barbara Marx Hubbard calls us the "crossover generation," here to lead the way from one stage of evolution to another. The following is her description of what we are evolving into:

> The universal human is one who is connected through the heart to the whole of life. Attuned to the deeper intelligence of nature, and called forth irresistibly by spirit to

creatively express his or her gifts in the evolution of self and the world. Above all, a universal human has shifted identity from the separated egoic self to the deeper self that is a direct expression of source.[2]

Hubbard's *universal human* is what many spiritual seekers strive to become through a process they call *ascension*. But what is ascension, and how does it differ from spiritual awakening, enlightenment, etc.? Indeed, is it even necessary to make distinctions between these terms? For the sake of clarity, let's take a look at this.

If you research "ascension," you will find multiple definitions. At one end of the spectrum, ascension simply refers to the slow and gradual progression of evolution we've been participating in for eons. It is considered our natural heritage as an evolving planet and species. Alternatively, in some circles, "ascension" refers to specific meditation or energy work practices.

Somewhere near the middle of the scale, and generally for our purposes here, ascension can mean undergoing a process of raising one's overall *vibration* or energy frequency through meditation or other spiritually uplifting practices. This can be considered a natural evolutionary process, but can also imply a lot of additional work and intention on the part of the aspirant.

Kryon, channeled by Lee Carroll, describes ascension as the opportunity to advance to your next lifetime without death. The ascended person has transcended his karma, fulfilled his contracts, and is fearless, nonjudgmental, and wise. He is not the person he used to be. He is an ascended being occupying the same body as before, although his body is now upgraded and enjoys a higher frequency by virtue of his spiritual vitality.[3]

There are other versions of ascension that say the body dies, or appears to die, but instead of going through the usual death process (which usually involves a multi-step reorientation process), the fully enlightened, ascending person *consciously* exits the body. The implication is that the ascended person's work as an incarnated being is complete; however, he may choose to return to earth as a helper or guide to others.

At the far end of the spectrum, ascension, also known as *assumption* or *translation*, is the circumstance whereby certain spiritually elite human beings enter heaven without dying or shedding their bodies. This is a belief held by many traditional religions, including Christianity, Judaism, and Islam, as well as many unconventional or mystic traditions. In these seemingly rare cases, the body undergoes a transformation by which its atomic structure is altered or its vibration is raised to where it is no longer comprised of matter, but has become pure energy. These high-vibrating *ascended masters* transition along with their now etheric bodies.

There is a belief that because of an evolutionary leap occurring on the planet at this time, the earth (including plants, animals, and human beings) is undergoing an ascension process whereby the nature of *time* is changing, our collective vibration and temperature are rising, and we are actually shedding density or transforming into light. This transformation into "lightbody" is what many spiritual seekers refer to as ascension.

Can this be possible, and what are the implications of such an evolutionary leap? While I cannot answer these questions, one thing for certain is that the scientific worldviews we have held for the last few hundred years are just that, scientific worldviews that contain many unanswered questions and even more unsatisfactorily *answered* questions about the nature of life. That said, even modern science and physics are now questioning the very nature of time, space, matter, and the idea of multiple dimensions. The universe is so huge, and its mysteries are so mind-bending that I'm going to ask you to suspend your previously held beliefs and make room for your *own* guidance to show you the way.

You have access to all the answers to your questions. So what is spiritual awakening to you? Is it the beginning, or closer to the end, of the road to enlightenment? And is that road itself the ascension process, or is ascension an *event* that occurs when enlightenment has been reached? Do you need answers to these questions, or are they just the ego demanding answers?

An Evolutionary Leap

Even with its apparent ups and downs, rises and falls, evolution has been a constant driver throughout history. Each generation serves as a foundation or building block for the next, and each evolutionary failure becomes the impetus for future success. Our children come in knowing things that we could not have known at their age, *being* ways that we could not have been at their age.

This is also true globally. The many crises we've been experiencing as a planet, the economic, environmental, and social breakdowns we are witnessing, serve as evolutionary drivers pushing us toward an improved existence. When we see something we don't like, our minds often create an improved scenario, which begins a concrete manifestation process.

For example, hearing about children dying from contaminated water supplies causes most of us to wish that these children had plenty of clean water to drink. While wishful thinking alone does not solve the problem, the seeds of desire planted by our *response* to this heartbreaking situation can provide the foundation for improvement and expansion.

Also, while mass media has tormented us with stories and pictures of violence and suffering occurring across the globe, it has also served to narrow the gap between ourselves and the rest of humanity. Deep in our hearts we know that we are connected, and for an increasing number of us, it is no longer possible to continue to ignore this simple fact.

While natural evolution has been ongoing throughout history, many believe that a major evolutionary *leap* is occurring on this planet right now. People are waking up en masse, and many children are now born in an already-evolved state. The kind of spiritual advancement that once required years of meditation, religious devotion, and/or psychotherapy is now much more accessible. Our sincere intentions and a willingness to embrace the present moment can now move us forward quickly.

You may be sensing that this is true and yet wondering how and why this leap is occurring at this time. While we will not engage in highly scientific explanations, let us consider the role of *cycles* and *alignments*.

On earth, each minute represents a sixty-second cycle, and each hour represents a sixty-minute cycle. Each twenty-four-hour period constitutes a cycle whereby the earth completes a full rotation on its axis. At midnight each day, these minicycles align and a new day begins.

Furthermore, approximately every twenty-nine days, the moon revolves around the earth and culminates in a full moon whereby the earth, moon, and sun are in alignment. Every 365+ days, the earth completes a full rotation around our sun. These and other cycles and alignments are significant to human life, and when they *converge*, change happens.

Apparently at this time, several vastly larger cycles are completing in our universe simultaneously, which is believed to be unprecedented. The completion of these cycles is converging in or right around the year 2012, which helps to explain why there has been so much attention placed on that particular year. Many consider 2012 to be not the end of time, but the end of a long era.

It is a time of endings and new beginnings, and many theorists and spiritual teachers believe that it is signaling a *golden age*, or at least new possibilities and potentials for planet earth. Some even believe that our entire planet is in the process of raising vibration and turning into light.

So what is all this 2012 excitement actually based on? Well, apparently the ancient Maya have proven themselves to be master spiritual timekeepers as well as astronomical and mathematical geniuses. They had multiple calendars and timetables for various purposes, such as agriculture, human gestation, moon cycles, galactic cycles, spiritual cycles, etc. They left many monuments that would help later civilizations interpret their calendars and prophesies, and although we have achieved this to a great extent, not all of the existing information has yet been revealed.

Like our modern-day calendar cycles, the Mayan cycles ranged from the very short to the very long. Their various smaller cycles, however, all converge in a "Long Count Calendar," whereby one Great Cycle equals 5,126 years, which represents the end of a *sun* or *age*. Five Great Cycles makes up a Grand Cycle, or 25,630 years. This represents a galactic cycle and measures the *precession of the equinox*, or the time it takes the earth to circle through all the constellations. This approximately twenty-six-thousand-year cycle is, in fact, corroborated by modern astronomical observation.

Somehow, around 200 BCE the Maya developed the Long Count Calendar, in which they set the start date (of the current era) at approximately three thousand years prior to that year. After extensively studying the calendars and prophecies, many researchers (but not all) have concluded that this calendar or era ends on Dec. 21, 2012. That represents not only the end of the 5,126-year great cycle, but the end of the larger 25,630-year galactic cycle. The belief is that this all represents the end of a *very* long era.

Furthermore, energy worker and channel Amorah Quan Yin writes that we are not only at the end of an approximately twenty-six-thousand-year cycle, but we are at the end of a 230-million-year cycle in which the entire Pleiadian system (including our solar system) orbits around the galactic center; *and* we are at the end of a considerably longer cycle in which our entire galaxy orbits around a "Great Central Sun." She goes on to explain that the end of a major cycle always includes a housecleaning phase, during which all unresolved issues, personal as well as planetary, are brought to the surface to be cleared.[4]

This, of course, is channeled information that cannot be proven, although science does confirm that it takes our solar system about 230 million years to circle the galactic center. Nevertheless, the message is clear: this is a time of great change. It is a time when cycles within cycles within cycles are lining up.

What will occur in the next few years or decades is unknown, but one thing is certain: change is in the air. We can fear it or embrace it, but from my point of view, it is a truly exciting time to be alive, and the fact that you are on the planet now means that you came here to be a part of it.

Many believe that this transition period represents a great window of opportunity for spiritual advancement, which is why many spiritual seekers are feeling the pull to heal their own issues and help other people, as well as the earth herself, do the same. Regardless of what happens or doesn't happen in the next few years, *now* is a great time to do your homework, unload your baggage, tune into your purpose, and become the person you came here to be. That is what this book is about.

TWO

In the Beginning

Y ou may still be wondering why we came here in the
first place. What soul in his right mind would give up a
beautiful, conscious connection with the divine, liter-
ally a heavenly existence, to experience a 3-D world where disease, crime, war, and misery are just normal parts of life? Who
would consciously choose such a fate, and for what possible
reason? What were we *thinking* when we agreed to forget who
we really are? And how could a loving God just stand by and
watch this suffering occur? These are the very questions that
led so many of us to abandon our Higher Selves in favor of the
ego, which at least attempted to protect us from a cruel world.

The Earth Adventure

Angelic channel Steve Rother describes how the "grand game
of free choice" originally began. The following discussion is
largely based on his explanation.[1]

Apparently source energy, or God, desired to *express* and *observe* itself beyond a pure energy state. To achieve this, sparks of this divine source would take form physically for the purpose of expression and would engage in relationship with other souls. In so doing, we would see our true selves, our godliness, through the eyes of others. This is exemplified in the phenomenon of *falling in love,* during which we get an intoxicating glimpse of our own and another's divine nature.

Souls, like ourselves, were presented with the opportunity to venture forth on an exciting adventure whereby we would attempt to transcend the illusion of separation from source. In this exercise, there would be elaborate veils that would prevent us from recognizing our true nature or that of other souls. We would forget our home, and most of us would believe that the props and disguises around us were real. Only the most adventurous and heroic souls would volunteer for such a difficult mission. It would span eons, but this would be a drop in the bucket to the eternal soul.

The exercise would be enacted in phases (incarnations), and between phases we would have the opportunity to return *home*, rest up, evaluate what we had just experienced, and make arrangements for the next phase. We would decide ahead of time many of the details of our incarnation, based on the lessons we most wanted to learn. We would select parents and a body, and we would make contracts with other souls as to the most important relationships and events that would take place to facilitate certain lessons.

These lessons would help us gradually remember who we are, and as more and more souls remembered, ideally we would achieve the ultimate objective of creating heaven on the physical plane, or spiritual ascension. We would step back into our natural roles as *conscious* co-creators with God.

Earth would not be the only game in town, but it would be unique in several important ways. First of all, humans would experience the maximum level of separation from source, which would plant the seeds for a fearful and potentially hostile environment. This environment would provide the ultimate challenges and rewards for courageous, ascending souls like us.

Next, we would be given *free will*. There would be minimal interference from the divine hierarchy. Within the boundaries of the spiritual laws of the universe, we would be given free choice in all matters. We would even be allowed the freedom to harm ourselves or others. Of course, this harm would be neither lasting nor real, but part of the many illusions and veils inherent in the game. Like a great movie or play transforms us, so would the experiences set forth by the game of free will.

Other necessary components of the earth experience would be *polarity* and *time*, neither of which exists on the other side of the veil. Here, we would perceive opposites: right and wrong, good and bad, young and old, life and death, past and future, us and them. Living in this *contrast* would be so stressful that it would cause massive wars, crime, hate, and so forth, but it would eventually help us define who we are and who we are not. Ultimately contrast would serve a positive, creative function.

We would have a family and social system whereby *special relationships* would be a way of life. For example, we would mate with other specially selected souls for the purposes of intimacy, reproduction, and child rearing. Our own children would be more important to us than other people's children. This would be built into our complex emotional fabric.

Even though this quality of specialness would seem "normal" to us, from a spiritual perspective of *oneness,* it would be both contrary and inherently problematic, for when we have special relationships and connection with certain people, we become extremely vulnerable to loss. This relationship piece alone would set up a tremendous fear matrix that would increase our separation from source even more.

While there would be many other unique conditions here on planet earth, suffice it to say that this human experience would intentionally set us up for a profound learning experience. While exceedingly challenging, this exercise of mastering separation and reawakening spiritually would be exciting, and there would be plenty of help available along the way. We would never be alone, even though we would often feel alone. Our higher aspects, the greater part of who we are, would be kept safe for the duration of the experience, so there would be no danger of us becoming permanently lost or damaged.

While technically we would always be connected to our Higher Selves, the trick would be learning how to consciously access our Higher Selves and the vast array of spiritual guides that would be available to help us at any time. For the most part, these spirit helpers would not be allowed to interfere with our free will, but would gladly step in if asked.

The earth experiment would have an expiration date, which is to say that we humans would have a certain amount of time to accomplish the objective of awakening and remembering who we are. Some believe this is reflected in the

Mayan calendar that completes in 2012, which indicates the end of an era, but does not necessarily indicate global death and destruction.

According to many ascension theorists, if a critical mass of humanity was able to awaken spiritually within the given time frame, we would advance to the next level of evolution, and a new golden age would begin, whereby separation consciousness would fade away, and heaven would eventually be created on earth. If not, as prophesied, there would be a seemingly catastrophic event that would cause us to leave our physical bodies and move on to our next experience of living. Either way, our souls would be fine.

Rother and other spiritual channels are of the opinion that this critical mass has, in fact, been achieved, and a new golden age on earth is in the making. This is not to say that a particular outcome is guaranteed, nor that anyone can predict with certainty what this new way of living will look like, but that it appears we have averted global destruction and will have the opportunity to move forward, if we choose. It should be noted, however, that many souls who have not contracted to stay for this new phase will choose to depart, and many already have.

The Hero's Journey

By now you are probably beginning to grasp the vastness and complexity of this human endeavor. Our lives represent layer upon layer of experience and meaning, and the journey we are on is truly heroic. This brings to mind the work of the great American mystic, Joseph Campbell.

Joseph Campbell spent years studying and comparing the mythologies of the world, and two of his favorite universal themes were the *Hero's Journey,* which is the story of humanity's quest for enlightenment, and the *Perennial Philosophy,* which says that the kingdom of God lies within each of us, or in Campbell's words, "You are the mystery which you are seeking to know."[2]

A hero is someone who has struggled through great adversity, lived through great pain, and been transformed by it. He or she, by definition, then uses this experience to help others.

Some modern-day Western myths that exemplify these themes are: *Lord of the Rings, Harry Potter,* and *Avatar.* In each story, we have a reluctant, would-be hero, an average sort of guy who for one reason or another finds himself in the unenviable position of having to lead the fight of good versus evil. In each case, the "hero" is outnumbered, overwhelmed, and ill equipped, but through perseverance, intent, and basic goodness is able to call forth that which is necessary to get the job done.

The truth is that we each have a story not unlike these, but uniquely our own. We are all heroes on a grand journey. It's not that we are fighting evil, but that we are fighting the illusion of evil, which is the backdrop of this stage set we call the human condition. Each time a hero conquers her fears (the illusions of separation from source) the angels sing, for there is no greater moment than when a soul returns safely home from battle.

When, in the midst of the scariest dream imaginable, we realize that there's no real danger, that we are invincible in our union with God, and that everything we needed we possessed all along, the universe lights up and expands in all directions. The birth of something new and beautiful takes place. *This* is what we came here for, and we *are* heroes.

THREE

The Unfolding of Consciousness

The stages of spiritual awakening, in various forms, can be found encoded within the teachings of many ancient texts, both Eastern and Western. Spiritual masters have walked among us throughout history and have given us glimpses of what evolved beings look like. While we have had access to their teachings for a long time, it is only recently that these truths have begun to speak directly to the masses, or at least to a critical mass of humanity.

Before this, spiritual teachings were converted into religions, and these religions then taught people what to believe and how to behave. In many religions, people were discouraged from seeking a direct relationship with spirit or inquiring within for spiritual guidance. In fact, during certain times in history, direct contact with spirit was considered *heresy* and was punishable by death, as was the case in the great inquisitions.

Not long ago, it was rare, at least in the West, for mere mortals to tap into the secrets of the universe or their own souls. In Europe, the early psychology works of Sigmund Freud and Carl Jung launched an era of exposing the internal conflicts of the human psyche, conflicts based on the existence of the ego, which is the driver of the lower aspects of self. It was found that the ego had a separate agenda from that of spirit and that the lion's share of our pain and suffering was caused, in one way or another, by the ego.

Now, several decades later, many of us are coming to realize what Jesus, Buddha, and countless other masters knew all along, which is that the ego merely shows us where the light needs to be shone. It shows us where we need to focus our healing. The ego made this earthly experience possible, and if we can reconcile and integrate ego with spirit, we can unleash tremendous co-creative power, and we will evolve, not just individually, but as a species.

The ego, while fragmented and fear based, can be elevated and rehabilitated. It can be transformed into the helping hands (and feet) of spirit. The ego is not our enemy any more than a rambunctious child is our enemy. Just as a nervous preschooler responds to loving kindness, so can the ego learn to respond to, and trust, the Higher Self, which is by its very nature loving. And just as a spirited teenager rebels against a controlling parent, so does the ego rebel when it feels that its authority is being overtaken, even by a benevolent Higher Self.

The delicate process of shifting authority from the ego to the Higher Self requires that the ego come to trust and honor the Higher Self. The ego must understand that the Higher Self does not mean to obliterate it, but to enlist the ego in a grander plan of safety and vitality than it could have orchestrated on its own.

For this to happen we must be willing to practice acceptance and forgiveness, for the habitual thinking and judging of the ego keeps us imprisoned in a dualistic world. When we begin to accept and forgive ourselves and others, the ego begins to loosen its death grip on life, and miracles of transformation occur. Inner peace becomes possible.

These miracles are only the tip of the iceberg, however, because we've been experiencing them for some time. Under the surface lie uncharted waters, new and exciting opportunities to step into our highest potential. Evolution is a self-transcending progression; it has the capacity to take us beyond our previous limits.

We might not know where the awakening process will lead us, but we know for certain that the time for change has come. We can feel it in the air. We can feel it in our bones. Those who resist this change are clinging to the old ways of the ego, and this can only bring about suffering, now more so than ever. You probably see this all around you, and perhaps even in your own life.

The immediate task before us is one of making a shift from ego to essence, and that is done by learning to listen to our divine inner guidance. This is all we've needed to learn all along, because our divine guidance is foolproof and always has the next step on our path laid out, even if that step involves waiting. Once we've begun to identify and trust our inner guidance, the rest are just details. Our true work is done.

This is not to say that every bit of guidance will lead us into a joyful situation, because sometimes it is our path to encounter bumps in the road that lead to greater learning or healing for ourselves and/or others. However, the Higher Self and your team of master guides and angels have an eagle's eye view of your path, and they can clearly see what is in your best interest *and* the best interest of others. We, by our very human nature, may be wearing blinders, but they are not. We may see only win-lose situations, but they see win-win situations and will guide us toward them, if we allow it.

Your ego might mean well, but since it is based on illusions of separateness and limitation, it cannot lead you to your highest good. Living from a place of ego is like living in a 3-D maze. You can't see where you're going or what's around the next corner. It is a bumper-car process of trial and error. The Higher Self, however, sits above the maze and can tell you when to turn left, when to turn right, when to stop, and when to go.

You might be thinking, "Well, that's cheating. It's not supposed to be that easy, and where's the challenge? I'd get bored." The challenge, of course, is learning to identify and trust your divine guidance, and only the ego believes that it shouldn't be easy, because the ego is accustomed to hardship and drama. There's little hardship and drama when we are following our inner guidance, because we know that everything we're experiencing is for a reason, and we feel supported by the universe. It's a different quality of being than feeling lost and alone, fearing for our very existence. It's night and day.

Every human being experiences loss, but how we perceive the loss is based on whether we're coming from ego or spirit. For the ego, loss of a loved one is a devastating tragedy and is further validation of our fearful and precarious stance. This can set the ego-based person reeling, perhaps for years.

On the other hand, a person who is consciously connected to spirit, while also subject to the grieving process, possesses *resiliency*. She possesses true inner strength and recognizes that death is only of the physical body. The soul never dies, and the relationship she shared with her loved one can never end. In fact, many people say that their relationship with a loved one actually improved after that person's death, but this is only possible if we learn to see beyond the veil.

As for excitement, there's nothing more exhilarating and magical than following the path of spirit. Synchronicities occur that positively blow your mind. The qualitative difference between living from spirit and living from ego is like the difference between sipping a glass of fine wine and chugging a plastic bottle of cheap vodka. Think about it, haven't we all had enough nasty hangovers? It doesn't have to be like that. Not anymore.

Stages of Spiritual Evolution

The process of personal spiritual development is a microcosm of the greater evolutionary process, for humanity and beyond. While many good models of these stages exist, sometimes the simplest can be the most effective at communicating where we've been and where we're going.

Reverends Michael Beckwith, Marcia Sutton, and Lloyd Strom are credited with the following model of the four Kingdoms of Consciousness.[1]

To Me: I am separate and powerless. I am at the mercy of that which exists outside of me. If there is a God, he may punish me.

By Me: As I step into my personal power, I am no longer a victim. I take responsibility for my life. I manifest my own reality.

Through Me: Spirit is a powerful force in my life, which I tap into regularly. I am guided and directed by my Higher Self, angels, etc. God works through me.

As Me: I am an embodiment of spirit. There no longer exists a distinction between higher and lower selves; all is healed and merged. This is "I Am" consciousness.

The following stages of spiritual evolution, which include the above kingdoms, are presented in a linear fashion, and while this process does tend to occur as a gradual progression over time, real life is rarely neat and tidy. We may jump around, regress periodically, get stuck, or appear to skip stages altogether. Some days and some years we may run the gamut, from top to bottom, so don't be concerned about where you or others are on the scale, because we are all constantly changing and evolving.

Stage One: Living the Unconscious Life

While we, as humans, are endowed with an egoic, survival-oriented self, as well as an essential spiritual self, at this stage of development the lower self is unaware of the Higher Self and lives without the benefit of this conscious connection.

At first the personality is highly fragmented and reactive. The mental, emotional, and physical aspects of the person are disorganized and out of alignment, and many problems ensue. The person is unaware of his role and responsibility in his own life. He is victim and/or perpetrator.

Through a process of trial and error and usually several lifetimes of experience, the soul begins to integrate the personality somewhat and may achieve a degree of success in his ability to run his own life. In fact, he may be quite functional and/or intelligent, but he is still unconscious of his Higher Self and is therefore self-limited.

Stage Two: Spirit Is Revealed

Through a series of crises, glimpses of latent spirit, and turning points, the unconscious person begins to conceive that there is more to himself and the world than he had previously imagined. A dramatic example of this is the *near-death experience*, in which we experience a vastly expanded view of our existence. Most of the time, however, people have subtler experiences that demonstrate the need for personal reevaluation of their belief systems and their place in the larger scheme of things.

Barbara Marx Hubbard and others refer to *a genius code* or *evolutionary code* that lies dormant within each of us and represents our inner spiritual potential. The genius code is a blueprint of sorts, and once activated, it acts as a driver in our spiritual awakening and evolution. The annunciation of one's genius code may come through unprecedented psychic or spiritual experiences that catch our attention and set us on a new course, or it may present itself in another way.[2]

Depending on how attached one is to his ego and his old way of thinking, this can be an exciting adventure or a threatening new development. Accepting the presence of spirit may be relatively easy and natural, or there may be tremendous denial and resistance that leads to round after round of internal struggle. Every time a candidate says "no" to his budding spiritual self, he is shutting the door to his greater power, and on some level he knows this. Fortunately, before too long Higher Self will knock again, and the person will have another opportunity to consider a spiritually inclusive approach.

Stage Three: Living in Two Worlds

There may be an initial period of excitement and wonder as we embrace a new world of possibilities, but eventually we feel the familiar pull of the ego. Because we are not yet firmly committed or established in our spiritual identity, we are in the precarious position of straddling two worlds. We will certainly have moments of thinking that the call of spirit was just a dream, that we only imagined things could be different. We may experience a yo-yo effect, and our self-image, career, and relationships may stand on shaky ground. What worked before may no longer be satisfying. At this stage, change is inevitable.

This is not an easy time and could be called a *dark night of the soul*. It may be a time of great confusion and crisis of identity. This experience, while initially acute, may recur as we go through many cycles of doubt and then resolution. In fact, it could be argued that the entire process of spiritual awakening, from unconscious being to embodiment of spirit, is a series of cycles of alternating spiritual illumination (which increases) and dark nights of the soul (which gradually decrease).

Stage Four: Conscious Evolution Begins

While the ego is still alive and kicking, at this stage we have turned the corner and are now committed to the path of spiritual awakening. We have fought many battles, become less identified with the material world and more identified with the world of spirit, and we have begun to release self-limiting behaviors and situations. We are learning to reconcile the internal and external forces of light and dark, realizing for the first time that we are responsible for everything in our lives.

This stage may bring about substantial changes in relationships, career, and other areas, but now we are more prepared to venture forth. Some friendships will end, while new ones are forged. A successful businesswoman might realize that she has not been following her passion and may set off on a new and uncertain course that others find utterly impractical. At this stage, we may become preoccupied with finding and/or fulfilling our divine life purpose.

Throughout this time, we are beginning to validate and accept our inner guidance, as well as seek instruction and guidance from teachers, books, etc. Our intention to know ourselves and self-actualize may call us to investigate mystic traditions or experiment with spiritual practices, such as meditation, yoga, journaling, etc.

Stage Five: Channeling Spirit

As our connection with Higher Self and the divine is felt more deeply, we become conduits through which divine inspiration flows. We may notice that our intuitive abilities gradually become more refined and we are able to pick up

31

more information about people and life by tuning into our own guidance. We may notice more synchronicities, or meaningful coincidences, going on all around us.

Most importantly, we are learning to choose the guidance of spirit over the guidance of the ego. In fact, ego is learning to defer to the voice of spirit, as it is now beginning to understand that spirit has its best interests at heart. This is a glorious development, as the resistance of ego begins to fade and spirit takes its rightful place as leader. Spirit is directing us and working through us.

Stage Six: Co-Creation

At some point in spiritual development (for some it is earlier, and for others, later), we begin to be drawn to other like-minded souls for the purpose of pooling our energy and intention for the greater good, even though we may not be consciously aware of this drive. For example, an introverted individual who has been meditating on his own for many years may feel the pull to join a spiritual group, prayer circle, cause, or volunteer organization.

By this stage, we recognize that we can change matter. During our private meditation as well as with like-minded others, we send prayers or light out to the rest of the planet. Ideally this is done in a pure fashion, without attitude or bias, because by sending pure light it can be used as needed and for the highest possible good. Any conditions or judgments we attach can only limit the outcome.

Often at this stage, we can feel the genius code at work within us, and through connecting with the genius codes of others, we experience a fusion, expanding the definition of *individual* to embrace the *whole*.

Hubbard writes, "Each level of genius is a facet of a whole essential reality. Through co-creation, each individual expands and reflects the sum of all the genius evoked by each co-creative partner. The actual co-creative project or result manifested through co-creation is secondary in significance to the unification and expansion of the collective awareness inspired by the process."[3]

Stage Seven: Embodying Spirit

Gradually the many aspects of lower self and Higher Self unite in such a way that spirit is no longer guiding us, but we recognize that spirit *is* us. We are no longer a conduit of spirit, but are spirit itself, embodied. This is perhaps the full state of spiritual awakening or enlightenment available at the human level.

From this place, we see ourselves as co-creators with the angels, ascended masters, and all other representatives of God. There is a remembrance of ourselves as eternal, universal masters. Whereas once we felt spiritually inferior or superior to others, we now experience the divine in all beings and all situations. We no longer see the world in terms of injustice and tragedy, victim and perpetrator, good and evil. Duality fades away in favor of the ultimate reality of divine love, of which we are all a part.

At this stage, we intuitively understand the body's cellular structure. Kryon (Lee Carroll) explains that by tuning in to our bodies interdimensionally we can work with our own DNA. We can heal our own bodies not by attempting to *remove* disease, but by *rewinding* biological circumstances to where we were before we manifested the disease. The trick is to make friends with *all* of the cells of the body and to enlist the wisdom of our DNA. This shift in body consciousness makes the lightbody aspect of ascension possible. This potentially takes aging and death out of the human picture.[4]

While this is not our final destination as spiritual beings, it may mark the end of our earthly involvement, depending on our specific spiritual contracts. While at this stage we are free to ascend this worldly reality, many souls choose to stay on in service of humanity. In Buddhism, these people are known as *bodhisattvas*.

Stage Eight: Uncharted Territory

At this time in history, humanity is at a unique turning point. As we have discussed, many believe that humankind and Mother Earth are completing a Grand Cycle and that a new golden age is afoot. There is talk of mass *ascension* (in all its colorful definitions) and wide scale transformation.

While this ascended state might sound universally appealing, and some might worry that they, or their loved ones, are not "ascension material," it should be noted that not every soul has contracted to experience a substantial ascension process at this time or in this way, and that is perfectly fine.

While every soul is ultimately on a spiritual ascension *track*, he may or may not be ready or willing to commit to making a significant shift at this time. However, most likely your soul group—your family, close friends, and other kindred spirits—are moving together on a similar track, and when one person takes an evolutionary step, the rest of the group is elevated as well.

This is why many *lightworkers*, or spiritual task force people around the world, are feeling pulled to release their mental and emotional baggage and raise their own vibrations. Even unconsciously, they know that in so doing they are aiding others (their soul groups, geographical neighbors, and all of humanity) in doing the same.

Getting There from Here

So backing up a few steps, how do we enlist the ego to cooperate in our spiritual evolution? How do we heal our many wounds? And how do we come to live from a place of spirit?

Many established paths are available, all of which have their strengths and their weaknesses, and then there are the paths that we fashion for ourselves, based on what speaks to us. While some would disagree with this advice, I encourage you to pick and choose what ideas work best for you. Formal religions and philosophies may hold great spiritual truths, but they may not answer all of your questions in a satisfying and lasting manner. Ideas that worked for you as a child might not work for you at age twenty, and what worked for you at twenty might not hold up during middle age.

Likewise, you might embrace some parts of a spiritual system, while rejecting others. The important thing is to check in with yourself about what resonates with your own truth, because what's true for one person might not be true for another.

The next three chapters explain and highlight some of the most valuable principles available for helping us along on our journey of spiritual awakening and finding inner peace.

FOUR

Moving From Fear to Love

*A*Course in Miracles[1] is a Christ-based, channeled teaching that calls itself a system of spiritual psychotherapy. *The Course,* as it is commonly called, is intended to gradually shift our thought processes from the fearful thinking of our ego to the loving stance of spirit. In fact, it is based on the premise that there are only two forces in the universe: *love* and *fear,* and of these two, only love is real. Fear is illusory, and there's no such thing as evil, because evil is nothing more than an extreme expression of fear. Darkness is simply the absence of light. Likewise, annoyance, anger, resistance, addiction, compulsion, confusion, envy, jealousy, greed, selfishness, depression, guilt, shame, or *any emotion that does not feel good* is an expression of fear.

Love, on the other hand, is the pure state of being that is our essence. Love is not a feeling, although we can feel the presence of love. We know we are in touch with our Higher Selves when we experience one of the many expressions of

love, such as contentment, joy, peace, freedom, grace, forgiveness, compassion, vitality, enthusiasm, optimism, clarity,
altruism, or *any emotion that makes us feel good*. You may be asking yourself if this applies to the "highs" we experience when
we use certain drugs or alcohol, have meaningless sex, engage
in addictive behavior, get even with someone who has hurt
us, etc. This is an important question.

Even though these experiences are not based on love, per
se, they can sometimes have the effect of temporarily lifting
you *toward* the state of love. However, sometimes they will
pull you down toward greater fear. While it's easy to delude
oneself, especially when engaging in a compulsive or addictive
behavior, if you take an honest look at the net result of how
the behavior effects your life over time, it will become clear
whether this experience is elevating you toward love or keeping you in fear. Sometimes a cigar is just a cigar, and sometimes it is the path to your destruction.

Honoring Emotions

As human beings, we are equipped with emotional bodies that
serve the purpose of guiding us on our spiritual path. What
this means is that when we feel positive emotions (love), it's
a sign that we're in alignment with our Higher Selves and
that we're going in the right direction. When we feel negative
emotions (fear), it's a sign that we are out of alignment with
our Higher Selves and that we're going the wrong direction,
or at least in the direction of increased suffering.

Due to our immersion in the polarity game, however, we
lost sight of that system of checks and balances and came

to believe that suffering was normal, unpredictable, and had nothing to do with whether we were on our path or not. While it's true that the human condition is fraught with challenges, someone who follows her *bliss* has a very different life experience from someone who wanders into the dark forest alone, without regard for the howling sounds in the distance.

The soul group "Abraham," channeled by Esther Hicks, presents a helpful tool: an *emotional scale* ranging from joy/ knowledge/empowerment/freedom/love/appreciation, down to fear/grief/depression/despair/powerlessness. In between these two extremes we find, in descending order, other emotional states, such as passion, hopefulness, boredom, disappointment, worry, anger, and the insecurity/guilt/ unworthiness.[2] If the lower end of the scale included *behaviors* associated with the emotions, you would see various forms of violence and persecution listed as well.

The scale represents the emotional range between love and fear. It is only a guideline, however, because emotional content varies dramatically from person to person. For instance, a habitual worrier has a different relationship with worry than someone who seldom experiences it.

At any given moment, you can find yourselves somewhere on your own personal emotional scale, and you can get a sense of which direction you need to go to get back to your Higher Self or your essential state of love. If you think of each emotion as having its own energy signature or *vibration,* it's easy to see that sometimes, for instance when we are in despair, we don't have access vibrationally to enthusiasm. There's just too large a gap to bridge, and we have to work our way up the scale, one step at a time.

Progress lies not in trying to jump from extreme fear to the highest experience of love in one giant step, although miraculous shifts in perception do sometimes occur. The idea is to work your way up the ladder whenever possible and to whatever extent possible. It could be argued that this, in and of itself, is a spiritual practice so powerful that it can take you all the way from spiritual poverty through the stages of awakening.

So how does this work? *The Course* says that every moment of our lives we are choosing between love and fear, and what we choose is what we believe is *real*. This was eye-opening for me when I first read it in the early nineties, because it meant that I could no longer live unconsciously. If I intentionally cut someone off in traffic, it was no longer a meaningless act. I had to deal with the fact that, at least in that moment, I had chosen fear over love. The Higher Self (love) would never do that.

Working your way up your emotional scale sometimes involves moving from one unpleasant emotion to another. For instance, you could be pulled out of depression by getting in touch with your anger, which for most people is a step up the emotional ladder. This is because depression is sometimes an expression of buried anger. Even if your husband prefers you depressed over angry, you are still better off doing primal scream therapy than sleeping eighteen hours a day. The anger might just bump your energy up to the next level. The anger might not be fun, but it represents progress, emotionally.

On the other hand, if you tend to be chronically angry, you need to get in touch with what's beneath it, so that you can elevate yourself from that stuck place on your emotional scale. Perhaps the real issue is feeling rejected or unloved. In this case, it might be helpful to talk to someone you trust about these feelings, perhaps a therapist of some sort. Chances are this will begin to shift the blocked energy, and you can move up to the next level, which might be vulnerability or disappointment, but again, this movement indicates emotional progress toward the state of love.

Abraham-Hicks recommends that whatever the emotional situation, if you open to *a better feeling thought* it will move you up the scale. Let's say you're upset with your husband because he won't agree to your plans for remodeling your run-down bathroom. You're feeling angry and powerless, and you even fantasize about having the work done while he's away on a business trip. You realize that you're going a little overboard emotionally, so you ask your guidance to help you find a thought that feels better. If you're *willing* to feel better, you might actually notice a progression of thoughts coming in such as this:

"He's always so cheap and controlling...well, I guess he's not *always* so cheap...at least we're not in debt like most of our friends...I really hate the way our shower looks, but at least it functions well...actually the shower is really spacious, and I've always sort of liked the faucet...we do have two fully functioning bathrooms...most people in this world don't even have running water or toilets...wow, maybe I'm being a little spoiled, throwing a fit because one of my bathrooms isn't *aesthetically pleasing*...I don't know, maybe I should let this go for now...eventually I want to have the work done, but I don't mind waiting a year...I'm sure he'll agree to that...he's usually pretty reasonable..."

In this real-life scenario, the woman went from feeling angry and powerless to experiencing actual appreciation for her husband and her bathroom, and this took only a few minutes. She worked her way up the scale, thought by thought. This was possible because she put her emotional state above her ego's need for control. It was more important to her to be happy than it was for her to win the argument. She relaxed and felt peaceful once she realized that her true power lay in her own perception of the situation.

The ego might have said, "Don't be a victim, fight!" But spirit said, "Relax, everything's fine." In *The Course* a miracle is defined as a shift in *perception*. Sometimes this happens all at once, and sometimes it happens gradually over time. Often miracles are made possible by forgiveness.

The Importance of Forgiveness

Forgiveness is the cornerstone of *A Course in Miracles*. Through practicing forgiveness of self and others, we retrain our minds to release painful thoughts and limiting beliefs. When we forgive, we are choosing love over fear. We are sending a message to the ego and to the universe that says, "My peace of mind is more important than *this*."

When your ego is complaining about what you or someone else has done, you might say, "That may be true, but I forgive her anyway," or "I may have behaved badly, but I forgive myself anyway." This cuts right through the litany of justifications for blaming or holding a grudge. It's not that you are condoning the behavior, because people do all sorts of unacceptable things; instead you're saying, "I'm not going to *carry* this with me. I won't let this *infect* my soul. I choose freedom from the bondage of unforgiveness."

That's what forgiveness does, and that's why it is so critical to our health, well-being, and spiritual growth. Until we grasp this profound truth, we're destined to "walk the maze." Forgiveness opens the door to our greatest freedom and aligns us with our Higher Selves. Whatever you have not forgiven is eating away at your body and soul right now. Are you willing to continue to let that toxic energy control you? The stubborn ego might say "yes," but the truth is that your Higher Self never condemned anyone in the first place.

Essence does not judge—essence only discerns. Source energy doesn't even *register* right and wrong. Duality exists only in the physical world and in the lower dimensions of the spirit world.

If you aspire to be truly *of the light,* you must practice the fine art of forgiveness, and you don't have to do it perfectly. I remember hearing Marianne Williamson model this thought by saying, "Just because I forgive you doesn't mean we have to have lunch, *yet.*" Just being willing to *consider* forgiving can be a huge step, because you are setting your intention, and intention is nine-tenths of the law.

FIVE

Living in the Now Moment

As previously mentioned, the present moment is the point of greatest power. Many spiritual traditions agree with this principle and are, in fact, based on the practice of maintaining focus on the here and now. Even the Law of Attraction teachings tell us that the central point of attraction/creation is the present moment. What you eventually manifest always comes from what you are thinking and feeling now. Luckily, if you don't like something about your life, you can begin the process of change by redirecting your energy about it now, in this creative moment. The trick is maintaining your new stance in each new creative moment, or at least more often than not.

The Role of Time

You've probably heard the saying, "There's no time like the present," but the reality is that there's no time *but* the present.

The future has not happened yet, and the past is but a memory. Memories are subject to intense distortion, and what you believe happened in your childhood, how you perceived certain situations, is probably different from what objectively occurred. What you remember and what your sibling remembers about the Christmas of '76 may be quite different.

As mind-boggling as it seems, modern science tells us that outside of our space-time continuum, time does not even exist. This implies that if you were on the outside of our universe, looking in, you would perceive all events throughout time occurring *simultaneously*. If space-time is indeed a *continuum*, then what is happening in this moment affects what *is* happening forty years ago, as well as forty years in the future. So when you heal an emotional wound in this moment, you are sending healing to yourself in all directions of time. Likewise, when you hurt yourself in this moment, you are sending pain to yourself in all directions of time. Since we're all constantly changing, it could be said that the past and the future are also changing, all the time.

This introduces the subject of *parallel realities,* which is a fascinating and mind-expanding concept. Angelic channel Tashira Tachi-ren explains that in our free-will-based existence we are able to make choices that are not in agreement with the will of our Higher Selves. While this is not the case for all life forms throughout the universe, we have chosen to experience free choice and work through the consequences of those choices. Whenever we make a choice that goes against our spirit, a parallel reality spins off that reflects what spirit wants for us. In this way, we are always maintaining the higher expression of who we really are.

Apparently we keep launching parallel realities until we begin to awaken, which is to choose the path of spirit. Tachi-ren writes, "As you awaken and begin to follow spirit, no new parallels are created, and those that were created from your earlier choices are being pulled back and merged. You are living in constant, daily merging of thousands of parallels on this planet. When all these parallels have merged, all you have left is the reality that reflects the path of Spirit from the dawn of creation."[1]

Now, whether or not you choose to wrap your mind around the idea of parallel realities, please consider the core idea that the past and the future are only *virtual* realities. They are not real in the same way that the present moment is real, which is probably why the twelve-step program philosophy of taking life "one day at a time" is so effective.

When we focus on what's real and what's happening today, we are in touch with our true power and our true essence. Not to mention that we are much more likely to be able to manage stress this way. If we're spending our time regretting the past and worrying about the future, which many people do, life can become overwhelming. When we keep our primary focus on today, we free the mind to relax and stay grounded. More often than not, today is manageable. And even if you "fall off the wagon," which we all do sometimes, tomorrow's another today, another fresh start.

So does this mean that we shouldn't think about or plan for the future? Should we just drift from day to day in a non-committal, nomadic, flower-child-like existence? Probably not. We live in a 3-D world that requires us to plan ahead. Eckhart Tolle makes the distinction between *clock time* and *psychological time*.[2]

Clock time is what exists for practical purposes. The world we currently live in demands (to some extent or another) that we conform to clock time, so that we may coordinate with others and make plans. It is in this way that animals and people throughout time and space "prepare for the winter."

Psychological time represents the ego's tendencies to fixate on the past and the future and to use time as a way to ward off contact with the Higher Self, or God. The ego does this because it believes that its own survival depends on keeping spirit out. In fact this is partially true, because when we eventually transfer authority from ego to Higher Self the ego loses most of its power over us.

Resistance Versus Acceptance

Ego understands that the present moment is the portal to spirit and, therefore, resists it. *Resistance* is the language of the ego, while *acceptance* is the language of spirit. Like nature, spirit accepts life on life's terms, and living in the present means ceasing the endless stream of judgments that the ego has taught us is normal.

We experience resistance every time we shout "NO" at the form life is taking. Many of us have made a career of doing this, which is sometimes appropriate to our life's purpose, but it can also take its toll on our mental, emotional, spiritual, and physical health.

Every time we complain about anything, we are resisting life. Every time we judge or reject anything, we are resisting life. Every time we fight with anyone, we are resisting life. Every time we project into the future or into the past, we are resisting life. Every time we are impatient, distracted, irritated, or intoxicated, we are resisting life, because life exists in *this* moment, not in some other, spruced-up moment, in a different time or space.

Being with whatever is happening now, without needing to change it, manipulate it, escape it, or condemn it, is what it means to be in acceptance. It doesn't mean that we have to like what's going on, but when we accept life in whatever form it takes, the internal war ceases and inner peace becomes feasible.

Perhaps you've noticed that this idea of unconditional acceptance of the moment flies in the face of the previous discussion, in which you were asked to always reach for a better feeling thought, for the purpose of upgrading your emotional state toward love. This is a valid argument, and one that I have personally grappled with. There is no easy way to reconcile this discrepancy gracefully except to say that there are many paths to enlightenment, and what works for one person may not work for another. I have found comfort in holding each philosophy close to my heart and applying that which seems most appropriate at any given time. The reality is that they are not as mutually exclusive as they at first appear.

For instance, I was once at my daughter's softball practice where one of the parents was behaving objectionably. For some time, I wrestled with my reactions. I was in an intense experience of resistance and pulled out every trick I knew to control and change the situation. I tried appealing, ignoring, reasoning, manipulating, you name it, but nothing "worked." The offensive person continued to offend. Finally, exhausted, I sat back and took inventory of my remaining options.

Since the situation didn't call for me to take extreme action, I decided that I either needed to accept the situation as it was, or I could reach for a better feeling thought.

Next something amazing happened. I realized that the better feeling thought I was seeking was, in fact, acceptance. They were one and the same. With this insight, I felt peace at last. Now, it might appear that a jump from anger to acceptance had occurred in one step, but actually the entire experience of getting upset, then trying this and trying that, and then stopping to reflect represented many small steps up the emotional scale. I didn't realize I was inching up the ladder, and I certainly didn't do it gracefully, but the end result was acceptance, which was a welcome solution. My ego would have enjoyed the satisfaction of "shutting the obnoxious guy down," but spirit was quite pleased with the outcome (and I didn't create any new karma). Next time, spirit assured me, I'd catch on faster.

After this experience, I no longer worried about which of the two spiritual practices was "right." I realized that, for myself, maintaining an open mind and following my own inner guidance was more important than plugging into a system, no matter how great the system was. For someone else, perhaps, adhering to a particular religion or philosophy would yield the best results. But it's important to appreciate that this, too, might change over time, and that would be okay.

Flexibility is a necessary component to being present in the moment. When we're attached to the way things *should* be or to our own personal worldview, we resist new or different ideas, and this ties us to the ego. Closed-mindedness is one of the ego's calling cards, and so is attachment to psychological time. So whenever possible, stay present in the now moment and accept life, instead of resisting it. Change yourself or your world if it's appropriate, but don't stay trapped in the little world of ego.

The Breath

Breathing, slowly and deeply, is one of the best ways we can anchor ourselves into the present moment. If you think about it, breath is life itself, because when we stop breathing our bodies die. The breath is our umbilical cord to source. One of the most powerful forms of meditation is focusing on the breath, just noticing the movement of air and the sensations that this creates in the body and mind.

Eckhart Tolle explains that breathing creates *space* in the mind by creating gaps in our habitual thinking. One or more conscious breaths, taken several times a day, can usher in awareness where there was no space for it before. While our breathing may initially be unnaturally shallow, controlled, or irregular, merely becoming aware of our breath will bring it back to a healthy and normal pattern.[3]

Taming the Mind

Meditation is a wonderful way to learn to just be. When we first start meditating or sometimes even after years of practice, we get to observe the ego firsthand. The lower self resists, complains: "I'm uncomfortable... there are too many distractions... the kids are making too much noise... this house is a mess...I have a million things to do...I can't relax...it's cold in here…I should be exercising…I shouldn't have eaten that donut…I forgot to pick up the dry cleaning…what's that *smell*?"

Being present in the moment means letting those thoughts and judgments float by like clouds, without grasping at them. The noises, the forgotten task, the agenda, the smell are all gifts to train the mind to settle down and focus on what's important. More often than not, what is most important is being aware of this moment and being in alignment with our Higher Selves.

I remember once seeing a *National Geographic*-style photograph of a yogi meditating in a sweltering cave in India, and he was covered with flies. Despite all odds, he looked comfortable and at peace. In Vipassana meditation, the practice of pure regarding, the meditator is asked to simply observe the mind and body, without interference and without moving the body. No fly swatting or stretching allowed. It's a rigorous practice that few westerners truly enjoy, but can teach us volumes about our inner landscape, even in one sitting.

There are many forms and methods of meditation with different objectives, but most strive to help us find inner peace and deeper understanding of ourselves, others, the world, and the divine. They help us release unwanted mental and emotional debris and gain clarity and stability. People who meditate regularly tend to be calmer and more balanced than those who do not.

If you need motivation to cultivate your meditation practice, read the memoir, *Eat, Pray, Love* by Elizabeth Gilbert. Part 2, the India section of the book, guides you through the author's four-month stay in an ashram whereby she is transformed from "monkey mind," reacting or bursting into tears at the slightest provocation, to "quiet mind," able to sit in peaceful silence for several hours a day. Gilbert's portrayal of her experience beautifully demonstrates the many benefits of meditation.

Likewise, the Dalai Lama makes an excellent point about the human mind that we westerners sometimes overlook completely. Our minds are untamed and vulnerable to all sorts of problems. Our minds are afflicted with negative thoughts that lead to disturbing emotions.

In speaking of the experience of Buddha Shakyamuni (Siddhartha), the Dalai Lama writes, "He found that all human beings undergo suffering, and he saw that we experience this unhappiness because of our undisciplined state of mind. He saw that our minds are so wild that often we cannot even sleep at night. Faced with this host of sufferings and problems, he was wise enough to ask whether there is a method to overcome these problems."[4] This question led to six years of intense meditation and contemplation, out of which came the profound Buddhist teachings, which center around training the mind.

The wildness of the human mind, like the wildness of a lion or tiger, is something that most of us have just taken for granted. Our uneducated attempts at dealing with it have included such tricks as applying harsh or manipulative *control* measures to ourselves or others; using alcohol, drugs, or food to *sedate* ourselves; falling prey to obsessive and/or compulsive behaviors in order to feel some tiny semblance of *orderliness* (which ironically can lead to an increased sense of chaos); and so on.

Eastern philosophies such as Buddhism, the Yogic tradition, Taoism, and Confucianism have addressed this issue much more directly and deeply than have Western philosophies. Thankfully we are now seeing the value of such practices as breathing, meditation, nonattachment, acceptance, and focusing on the now moment. These are indispensable tools for spiritual awakening and developing inner peace.

Being in Resonance

When a singer or a musical instrument reaches a state of *resonance*, the sound produced becomes richer, fuller, and more powerful than before. It can reach inside us and move us because of the precision with which it is "hitting the mark."

The same concept applies to us when we are enjoying a moment of full presence in the here and now or experiencing resonance with our true nature. You may be able to recall times when you felt completely in alignment with life, your Higher Self, and God. Maybe you were meditating, sailing a boat, dancing, or enjoying an intensely happy moment with friends or family. Looking back, you know that you were tapping into the joy of *being*, which is your birthright, your natural, spiritual state.

Sadly, some people live in such a continuous state of low-grade fear and diminished expectations that these fleeting moments of true alignment only make them nervous. They are afraid to get their hopes up. When any little fear enters the picture, they can be knocked off balance, but through simple observation, we can all learn to identify where we've gone wrong and get ourselves back on track.

Beverly Ann Wilson, a spiritual teacher in Mt. Shasta, California, teaches the following principles. She says that you know you are out of resonance when:

1. You are living in the past, or living in the future.
2. You are not grounded enough, or you are too grounded (inadequately anchored and flying away, or overly rooted and can't soar).
3. You are being less than you are, or trying to be more than you are (playing too small or playing too big).
4. You are not pushing yourself enough, or you are pushing yourself too much (sluggish and inactive, or busy and overextended).

When you find yourself unhappy or out of sorts, try checking the above list. Chances are you will find yourself in one or more categories, but by applying a little focused intention to the situation, you may find that you are able to come back into resonance surprisingly quickly.

SIX

Following Your
Own Guidance

While the previous two chapters focused on transforming the mind, here we will focus on the subtler practice of self-referral, or going *within* for direction. This is important because in our culture, as well as many others, people are taught to look to the outside for guidance. There are "experts" for every subject: relationships, parenting, finances, education, health and fitness, etc. But these experts and well-meaning friends and family members do not have access to our divine life plan. Most of them have no way of understanding what lessons we have contracted for or from what paths we may benefit. For example, a parent might protect a child from the very rejection the child contracted to work through.

Another person's guidance is usually based on his own unique frame of reference and may serve only to confuse or mislead us, especially when we solicit multiple opinions that conflict with each other. Any information or advice we receive should be weighed against our own intuition. If it resonates or feels right, then we know we can trust it. If it doesn't ring true for us or feels wrong, then we should disregard it. This kind of *discernment* applies to everything in life, from the praise or criticism we receive to the information we read in books to the insights of our guru.

For example, several years ago I read a spiritual book that resonated so completely with my own inner guidance that when I read a crucial paragraph that did not fit for me, I began to question the premise of the book. I checked in with my guidance about it and was advised to "just ignore that part." A couple years later I learned that I, along with thousands of other readers, had misinterpreted that passage to mean something different than the author intended, and the issue was resolved.

You don't have to throw out the baby with the bath water. Instead you can choose to take what feels true for you and let the rest go, preferably without judgment. If something doesn't speak to you, it just means it was written or said for someone else.

You may be thinking, "Well, that sounds fine, but I'm not naturally intuitive like some of my friends. How am I supposed to *check in with my guidance?*" Psychologist and "Angel Lady" Doreen Virtue teaches that we are all naturally intuitive, but that our egos and other life circumstances sometimes mask these natural abilities. For instance, most young children can see angels or other spirit guides, but when their parents can't see these friends and label them "imaginary," the child begins to question whether or not they really exist. In fact, some children are even punished for *lying* when they report these or other psychic experiences.[1]

As adults, our intuition may be blocked, or we may disregard the insights that are coming through. We may pass them off as "just my imagination" or coincidence, or we might even be tapping into fear from a past life experience where we were burned at the stake or suffered some other horrific fate because we were in touch with or expressed our intuitive gifts.

As human beings, we are prewired for connecting with our own, foolproof guidance system. When we access that wellspring of knowledge, inspiration, intuition, and guidance, healing can occur, and we can create heaven for ourselves here on earth, while supporting others in doing the same.

In order to access this spiritual bounty, we need to learn to distinguish between the many voices of the ego (which tend to be louder) and the subtler voices of spirit (which include your Higher Self, angels, ascended masters like Jesus, Yogananda, and Kuan Yin, as well as other divinely sanctioned spirit guides).

At first this can be difficult, because the ego doesn't want you to tune into your higher guidance and can masquerade as spirit, or it can become so loud that you can't hear the voice of spirit. Don't be discouraged, however, because this gets easier with practice, and eventually you will experience a reversal: the subtle voices of spirit become more dominant, while the bolder voices of the ego become quieter and less demanding, like children whose needs are finally being met. (It should be noted here that we are referring to the "normal"

internal voices experienced by most people and not the psychotic voices heard by people with certain mental illnesses).

Generally speaking, you can distinguish between ego and
spirit by the way the voice makes you *feel*. The guidance of
spirit is loving, supportive, usually gentle, nonjudgmental, and
positive, even when warning you of danger. Spirit-based messages are consistent and repetitive and encourage forgiveness,
gratitude, win-win situations, being present in the moment,
and fulfilling your life purpose. The voices of spirit make you
feel confident and secure.

On the other hand, the voices of the ego, which also
sometimes reflect the influence of darker energies from the
outside, can have an immature tone and be quite judgmental,
competitive, and selfish. This guidance can feel cold and is
full of rationalizations. The voices of ego encourage worry
and blame and are fraught with complaints and impulsiveness.
Ego voices can be demanding and abusive and can encourage
you to behave rashly before you've had a chance to consider
options or weigh consequences. They tend to focus on the
past and the future.

Facing Your Inner Demons

Sometimes we are afraid to look within for guidance for fear
that we won't like what we find. Many of us have been programmed to feel ashamed of ourselves or to be fearful of
our inner rage or other emotions. Some of us are afraid that
we would find nothing but a worthless, stupid, or mediocre
person residing within. Whatever the reason, many of us take
great pains to avoid looking at ourselves. The irony is that

when we avoid facing ourselves, we tend to behave unconsciously, from the *default* guidance of our lower selves. This makes us more likely to behave poorly toward ourselves and others.

Likewise, when we are only semiconscious of our fear, and nightmares come to call, we may be jolted into looking at what brought them about. This is one of the purposes of dreams: to show us where we are on the path, where we need to make adjustments, and where we might be headed if we don't.

An example of this is the following dream, reported by a sophisticated psychotherapy client:

"In the dream, I'm being drawn into a cave where I believe something terrible is happening. I'm extremely afraid, but I know I have to go in. With me, I carry a flashlight, and what I see is horrific. There are children, whom I presume to be dead, lying all over the floor of the cave. Beyond them is a crazed madman, whom I call "the maniac." When I shine the flashlight on him, he begins to shriek, and he runs to get away from the light. Like the Wicked Witch of the West fears water, the maniac fears the light. He believes that his strength lies in the darkness. As I have the advantage, I chase him down and continue shining the flashlight on him until, unexpectedly, he begins to cry. I realize that the "maniac" is actually afraid, and he is deeply ashamed of what he has done.

"About this time, I begin to notice movement all around me. The children have begun to stir. They aren't dead after all. The *light* has brought them back, and they are unharmed. When the man, no longer a maniac, realizes this, he cries out in gratitude. It's as if he is transformed by the light, and together we all file out of the cave into the bright light of the day."

This dream was an invitation to go within, to face the fear, the madness, the shame, and the wounded inner children of my client's psyche, because they had not been doing well in the dark recesses of her mind.

This is true for all of us. Unhealed places must be bought to the light if they're to be healed, but this doesn't mean that we need to go digging around to find them. One of the great attributes of the human psyche is that it will present to you what needs to be healed. All you have to do is pay attention. If you repeatedly ignore messages from your inner guidance, issues begin to fester.

Generally speaking, illness, anxiety, rage, depression, weight issues, addictions, obsessions, compulsions, violent thoughts or behavior, etc., are all signs that we're not listening to our inner guidance and that this repression of self has progressed to the next level. Don't feel alone. We've all been there, and most of us still struggle with at least one long-standing issue that has its roots in repression and avoidance.

The hidden blessing in the most painful life experiences is that they force you to wake up and take inventory of what you've been doing or what you've been avoiding, and it's never too late to turn within. Even if you're on your death-bed, you can experience healing by going within and making friends with who you really are. Even if you're serving a life sentence in prison, it's not too late to turn your life around. Your Higher Self still loves you no matter what you've done and hasn't given up on you. Even if you have abandoned your spouse, your children, and yourself in this lifetime, spirit will never abandon you.

Using Your God-Given "Lifelines"

You may have seen the game show, *Who Wants to be a Millionaire?,* in which contestants are allowed to make a phone call to someone on the "outside," whom they hope can help them answer a question that will enable them to advance in the game. This is called a "lifeline."

We humans have been equipped with a vast array of channels, or lifelines, between our earthly selves and universal source energy. Many of us are unaware that these resources exist, or we do not recognize them as such, and end up feeling hopelessly alone and vulnerable in a big, threatening world.

Spiritual awakening is the process that illuminates these lifelines, and these divine channels are what make spiritual awakening possible in the first place. As mentioned before, we came here to lose our way and then find it again, and we do this is by discovering these lifelines, which are like clues that lead to the big treasure at the end of the hunt.

So what are we talking about exactly? These umbilical cords to spirit that we have already discussed include: the Higher Self, the emotional guidance system, forgiveness, discerning minds that are able to self-transform, following one's bliss, the breath, the present moment, meditation, dreams, etc.

Next we will explore several of the other lifelines available to us on our journey of awakening. Some of these will be familiar to you, while others will feel foreign. Some will seem important to you while others may appear superfluous. Some will strike you as ancient wisdom, while others you might dismiss as pop-occultism or New Age "woo-woo." As always, this information is presented for your personal discernment.

Channels of Intuition

As human beings, we possess physical senses that have their energetic counterparts. We see, hear, taste, smell, feel, and "know"; therefore, we can and do receive intuitive information through these senses. Depending on what our natural strengths and interests are, we can develop and learn to trust these channels of guidance.

Each of us has access to all forms of intuition, but we tend to be stronger in one or two areas. For instance, a photographer *sees*, a musician *hears*, a poet *feels*, and a scholar thinks, or *knows*. However, the musician might also be a strong feeler, and the scholar might have a developed visual sense. Our four main intuitive channels are clairvoyance, clairaudience, clairsentience, and claircognizance.[2]

Clairvoyance is "clear seeing" and can involve having memorable and vivid dreams or visions. You may see auras, flashes of light, colors, geometric patterns, or disembodied beings, with your eyes open or closed. You may have a naturally active imagination and may easily be able to invoke scenes and images in your mind's eye. You may have a somewhat photographic memory, remembering things that you've seen or read more easily than you could remember music or physical sensations you've experienced.

You may receive intuitive flashes or visions of yourself or others that represent where people have been or where they are going on their current path. Information and guidance might come in any of the above forms or might come from the imagery in films, beautiful scenery, photographs, or objects that you encounter in your environment.

Clairaudience is "clear hearing," and this hearing can emerge as words, music, or other sounds that seem to come from outside your head or as gentle and loving messages inside your head. These are not to be confused with the courser voices of the ego or the delusional voices sometimes heard by the mentally ill.

Clairaudient guidance can come when you "accidently" overhear a conversation that holds special meaning for you or when you turn on the radio just in time to hear something that you needed to hear. Messages can come through song lyrics or the way the music affects you in other ways. You may hear your name or another word called out as you are awakening from sleep, or you may hear a word repeated in your mind, like "forgiveness," which has obvious meaning to you, or possibly a word or sounds that you do not understand. You may find that humming, singing, or playing a musical instrument helps you feel more connected to your soul or others.

Clairsentience is "clear feeling" and involves emotional or physical feelings. Clairsentient people tend to be very emotionally sensitive and empathic, as well as particular with regard to environmental conditions, foods, fragrances, scratchy fabrics, tightly fitting clothes, other people's moods, etc. They can pick up on the *vibe* of a person or environment, usually with great accuracy, and become uncomfortable, overwhelmed, or even sick when they are in the presence of energy that doesn't agree with them.

For instance, a clairsentient who enters a house where there has been violence may feel a panicky need to get out as quickly as possible, while not specifically understanding why. Clairsentience is most often experienced through physical and emotional feelings, and sometimes through "imagined" smells or fragrances, air pressure changes, breezes, or a sensation of being touched, as on the shoulder or head.

Claircognizance is "clear knowing" and is experienced through thoughts, ideas, revelations, or knowledge that seems to be downloaded into the mind. You might find that when asked a question you suddenly know the answer even though you hadn't known it before, or that the answer unfolds gradually. You might notice that as you write, a stream of information or wisdom flows from your pen as if someone else had written it and that journaling is effective for you. People who have more access to claircognizance tend to be mental types: thinkers, readers, writers, professors, engineers, scientists, and inventors, and they just know things without having studied them.

For instance, my husband is a Ph.D scientist/engineer with a fairly strong intuitive sense. When asked virtually any question, if he's is interested in understanding the topic, a process begins whereby the answer is revealed to him. His response will sound something like this: "Oh, I don't really know…well, it's related to…okay, here's how it works…," and he'll answer the question in great detail as it is being *downloaded* to him. For years I thought he was just "making stuff up," but then I realized that he was almost always right.

People who value intuition become more and more intuitive and can be well versed in all of the "clairs." They find that life is much easier and more fun when they follow their own guidance and that they make few poor decisions. On the other hand, those who reject their hunches and gut feelings in favor of the egoic, rational mind often find themselves becoming more and more rigid and disconnected from their instinctive nature. They miss cues and red flags from people and from their environment and make many poor, if not disastrous, life choices. If you want your children to be safe, help them develop and exercise their intuition. Ultimately you cannot protect them, but they can protect themselves.

Prayer

While meditation is viewed as communication *from* source or simple observation *of* source, during prayer we generally speak *to* source. There are many different types of prayer, some formal and ritualized: "Our Father, who art in Heaven…" Others are informal: "Yay, God!" Some prayers have a beseeching quality: "Dear God, *please* help me…" Others are affirmations: "Mother/Father God, I see myself healed and whole…" Some prayers employ bargaining tactics: "If you make my wife stay, I promise to…" And some prayers are pure expressions of gratitude: "Praise the Lord!" Sometimes we ask for information or a sign from above.

Some people believe that we shouldn't "bother" God with petty concerns, because he is, or should be, busy taking care of *real* problems: "*I'll* find my own parking space—*you* stop the war in Iraq," while others believe that source can be everywhere at once and the more we connect with it, the better.

Some people are more comfortable addressing their prayers to angels, Jesus, Mother Mary, or other divine representatives because these figures feel more accessible to them: "Angels, surround me now."

While there's no right or wrong way to pray, I personally have found the most benefit from just speaking freely, but respectfully, with God, angels, and other spiritual guides often throughout the day. I find that the more I engage with them, the more they engage with me, and the more connected I feel to the divine. I ask for help whenever I need it, express all of my feelings and concerns, surrender whatever feels overwhelming, and offer gratitude regularly. In fact, my two favorite little prayers are: "I surrender this to you, God," and "Thank you, God."

Spirit Helpers

Most people are familiar with angels, and the majority of cultures and religions hold strong beliefs in various forms of spiritual helpers. While I've always believed that we have personal spirit guides, I didn't know what to make of angels. I didn't remember seeing them as a child, and while I remember having an imaginary friend named "Mo," he didn't really look angelic. My Protestant church didn't mention angels except at Christmas time, and neither my family nor friends ever spoke of them. Like fairies, I thought that angels were beautiful, mythological beings, predominantly symbolic in nature.

All that changed several years ago when I heard a talk given by an emergency room physician. Apparently, a few years before that, he had begun seeing and conversing with angels in his ER. These angels were either advising him on how to save a patient's life or assisting the patient in making her transition out of the body. The story was fascinating because this Western doctor was no "airy-fairy" guy. He seemed quite grounded and reputable, very scientist-like, and not at all prone to hallucinations.

I bought his book, devoured it, and then went out and read every other book I could find on angels. I started conversing with them, and before long, I was receiving a great deal of information and guidance from them. After studying with Doreen Virtue and getting certified in Angel Therapy®, I began doing intuitive work with individuals and teaching classes on connecting with our angels. Needless to say, I became a believer, and I continue to work with these divine beings every day.

While some people have concerns that we might be worshipping angels, instead of God, it is clear to me that all spiritual guides, including angels, are God's representatives, or task force, if you will. When we work with spiritual helpers and guides, we are connecting with God, or source energy.

We can communicate with angels and other high-level spirit helpers any time we like. We can ask for guidance, assistance, or help by writing, speaking, or simply thinking of them. We don't have to worry about bothering them, because it is their job to help us, and since they tend to be multidimensional and are not restricted by space or time, they can be in many places at once.

This is particularly true for the archangels, ascended masters, and other high-level beings. While spirit helpers will happily help us *when asked*, they cannot interfere with our free will. Only if we are in mortal danger before our time will they intervene without our consent.

While source energy or pure spirit is *undifferentiated,* spirit helpers (like our own souls) carry energies that differentiate or distinguish them from others, almost like the personality differences among people. Keep in mind that not all disembodied beings are *of the light,* and that's why it is a good practice to ask that only the highest, divinely sanctioned beings of light assist you. When seeking guidance, always visualize yourself surrounded with light, and if ever an energy does not feel right, ask it to leave.

This brings to mind a story about *Saint Anthony,* who, during a silent retreat in the desert, was reportedly visited by a host of angels and devils, some of whom resembled their opposites. When asked how he could tell who was who, he advised that the best way to distinguish a being's true nature is to notice how you feel *after* the being has left your side.

This excellent advice goes not only for angels and "devils," but for anyone or anything that you are exposed to. You may be confused or seduced while under the influence of someone or something, but checking in with yourself about it later will help you put things into perspective.

Know that you, as Higher Self or a spark of the divine, possess all the guidance you need. Teaming up with some of the following spirit helpers may provide spiritual assistance, but try to avoid the temptation of deferring to them or becoming dependent upon them. Their guidance serves as a stepping-stone as we learn to merge with our Higher Selves.

The following is a breakdown of some of the many spirit helpers available to us.

Archangels are overseers of other angels. They are bigger, more powerful, and more advanced than the other angels.

They are nondenominational, which means that they will help anyone, regardless of their culture or background. Archangel Michael is the angel of protection, Archangel Raphael is the angel of healing, Archangel Gabriel is the angel of communication, etc.

Guardian angels are contracted to be with a particular person, side by side, for that person's entire lifetime. Regardless of faith, belief, or lifestyle, we each have one or more guardian angels, and their job is to comfort, gently guide, and protect us to whatever extent possible, while respecting our free will and karmic agreements.

Specialized angels are available for any need that we might have, be it with regard to relationships, life path, career, parenting, protection, health, beauty, birth, death, grieving, etc. When we ask for angelic assistance in any area of our life, we will attract the help of these angels.

Ascended masters are highly enlightened beings who have walked among us, in human form, as great healers, leaders, or teachers. Even though they have "graduated" from earth, they love us and have so much compassion for us that they continue to help us from their ascended place in the spirit world. Like angels, they tend to have areas of special interest or expertise. Some of the better-known ascended masters are Krishna, Jesus, Mother Mary, Saint-Germain, Buddha, El Morya, Melchizedek, Kuthumi, Babaji, Yogananda, and Moses. Some, but not all, of the ascended masters can have a more intense energy than the angels, who naturally tend to be soft and comforting.

Deities, gods, and goddesses are found in many cultures, religions, and myths and are referred to here as energies or aspects of God. The goddesses represent the divine feminine, and while powerful in their own right, they often exemplify the subtler, *yin* energies of nurturance, creativity, etc. Goddesses also represent the life cycle archetypes of maiden, mother and wise woman, or crone. The gods represent the divine masculine and usually express *yang* qualities that are, by nature, more extroverted. Gods also represent the archetypes of young man, father, and wise old man.

This group also has special areas of interest, as well as personalities, and can help us when called upon. Like ascended masters, but even more so, these deities sometimes have passionate personalities. For instance, the Hawaiian goddess Pele, can be downright fiery, so do your homework and exercise discernment when calling on them. Some popular examples include Devi, Ganesh, Hathor, Thoth, Horus, Ishtar, Kuan Yin, Aphrodite, Maat, Pele, Athena, and Shiva.

Elementals are nature spirits that are found in and around earth, air, fire, and water. They range from simple and lower-vibrating spirits, lacking in intelligence and appeal, to beings that are beautifully complex, higher vibrating, and intelligent. While they have many names and classifications, like gnomes, undines, and sylphs, the generic term for nature spirits is *fairies*. As such there are earth fairies, garden fairies, mountain fairies, water fairies, air fairies, fire fairies, storm fairies, etc., and within these categories, the variations are endless. Nature spirits tend to the earth and animal life in the same way that angels and other spirit guides tend to human beings.

Because we are connected to and very much a part of Mother Earth, we can and do interact with elementals all the time, whether we realize it or not. Because human beings, especially in recent history, have disregarded and damaged the environment, nature beings do not always appreciate us.

The good news is that when we do demonstrate our love and respect for the earth these beings will serve as allies and assist us greatly in our lives and our spiritual growth, especially those of us whose spirituality is connected to nature. When you ask for guidance from and connection with the nature realm, your life will take on a grounded, yet magical quality that you might not have experienced before, or perhaps not since you were a child.

Galactic emissaries of light are benevolent beings not of this world who have agreed to help us in our quest for spiritual awakening and growth. Our connection to all of life goes beyond our own planet, which is just a tiny speck in a vast local universe. Our tendency might be to think of beings from other parts of the universe in terms of hostile aliens, flying saucers, abductions, and movies with really poor special effects, but it is valuable to step away from the stereotypes for a moment and consider the possibility of the richness, depth, and breadth of life outside of our own planet and solar system. Ultimately we are all visitors of earth who originated somewhere else in the universe; thus we are all aliens.

Because of the great ascension movement and evolutionary leap taking place on this planet right now, many intuitive teachers perceive extra help and guidance coming in from the outside universe. They see this as coming from the angelic realm as well as other benevolent galactic representatives of star systems like Pleiades and Andromeda, and the collective body known as the Galactic Federation. While much of this influence is *of the light*, or God sanctioned, we should always exercise caution when dealing with or invoking any guidance whatsoever, be it human or otherwise.

Miscellaneous Lifelines

The list of methods for tapping into spirit is endless and varies greatly from person to person, culture to culture. The following is an overview of a few more lifelines that people have found helpful.

Divination tools are ancient systems that have helped people, throughout history, connect with divine guidance. This is done in a variety of ways and to varying degrees, depending in part on the structure of the system, but in each case, interpretation plays a key role. We use and develop our intuition by stepping into the system and allowing its language to speak through us. The system can become a natural channel for our intuition to flow forth.

A few examples of divination tools are oracle cards, astrology, numerology, I Ching, runes, and palmistry. These systems and many others can help us plug into our own internal guidance.

Journaling is to some people what making art or music is to others. It is a way of expressing and sorting through feelings, thoughts, and ideas. The page is a safe place for ranting and raving, feeling difficult emotions, and working through stuck energy. It is a place where the many voices of ego and spirit can be heard. A journal can be a good friend with whom one shares everything. In fact, a journal can represent our relationships with all aspects of self.

Journaling is not just writing. It is writing infused with the intention of knowing oneself and moving forward emotionally or spiritually. Journaling can help us know ourselves on every level accessible to humans, which serves our process of awakening spiritually and finding inner peace.

For many people, the mere act of putting pen to paper can open channels and create miraculous connections, but this is not true for everyone. I've heard many people (including two published authors) say that journaling is not helpful to them. If this is the case for you, don't force it. There are plenty of other ways to know yourself and open to divine guidance. But if it does work for you, journal often, because it can be an extraordinary tool.

Energy work is a broad category that includes anything we do, think, or visualize with the intention of affecting energy. This includes prayer and meditation. A powerful energy worker friend of mine likes to say, "If it's energy, you can change it, and everything's just energy." Even though we live in a 3-D world where energy creates what appears to be solid matter, nothing is really as solid or unchangeable as it seems. For example, there have been countless cases, many documented, where people diagnosed with terminal illnesses experienced miraculous healings because of some application of energy work, by themselves or others.

A few other examples of energy work include the creative visualization practices associated with the law of attraction, Reiki and Therapeutic Touch, some forms of massage, chakra work, biofeedback, HeartMath, guided meditation, primal scream and other cathartic therapies, hypnosis and hypnotherapy, breath work, rebirthing, affirmations, decrees, light wave therapy, soul retrieval and other shamanic practices, color therapy, fasting, and so on.

Many of the above practices are utilized for the purpose of energy *clearing* and/or *shielding*. As human beings, we tend to unwittingly absorb and build up psychic and energetic debris, much of which can be quite toxic. Some of this comes from our own thoughts and feelings, while other toxic energy comes from outside of us.

Regardless of the origin, if not released or cleared, this energy can wreak havoc on our bodies and minds. In fact, many people believe that all diseases, even the genetically based sort, are caused by accumulated toxic energy. While there is widespread resistance to this theory, for our purposes suffice it to say that stress, resentment, unforgiveness, habitual negativity or pessimism, hatred, guilt, shame, regret, and other people's negative energetic influences do not do us any good and should be cleared on a regular basis.

How do we do this? There are many ways to clear energy, and some of them are as natural and intuitive as taking a deep breath, sighing, screaming, jumping up and down, going for a run, crying, surrendering to God, singing, venting to a friend, writing, taking a walk through the forest or on the beach, or petting your dog. Nature, which includes animal life, has a way of pulling toxins right out of us.

Other more elaborate clearing practices not previously mentioned include spinning chakras, cutting cords of fear, blowing roses, using the violet flame, etc. These methods can be effective and will be explained in part 3.

What Blocks Higher Guidance?

We have discussed a number of factors that either enhance our ability to hear inner guidance or inhibit us from tuning in. The following is a summary of several of the conditions that block this guidance from coming through.

1. *Worry,* or any habitual thought or preoccupation that consumes our time and energy focusing on problems: weight issues, safety issues, aging, health issues, relationship issues, money issues, etc.

2. *Addictions, compulsions, and obsessions.* When we're out of touch with our Higher Selves or higher purpose, we can feel lonely, depressed, anxious, empty, or confused. Often people develop a negative attachment to something or someone in an effort to fill the void or medicate/suppress feelings. Food, drugs, alcohol, sex, shopping, certain relationships, rituals, or thoughts can be used to fill the "God-shaped hole" in us.

3. *Ego focus.* The ego, which thrives on fear, blame, competition, and judgment, is a natural saboteur of our connection to higher guidance, peace, and love. The ego keeps us trapped in our heads and in our circumstances.

4. *Poor diet or eating habits.* Eating "dead" or overprocessed foods tends to deaden our receptivity to inner guidance, while eating fresh, alive foods strengthens our connection to source energy.

5. *Inadequate breathing* inhibits the circulation of spirit. Holding our breath or breathing shallowly prevents higher guidance from flowing naturally.

6. *Thinking too much.* While higher guidance sometimes comes in the form of a thought, it does not come as a result of processing thoughts and information. Higher guidance slips into our minds through the gaps in our thinking, which would explain why we get our best ideas while exercising, meditating, etc.

7. *Drama.* The habitual pattern of attracting drama and crisis comes from being out of touch with our Higher Selves. When we are in the high-vibrating flow of spirit, we feel exhilarated and alive, but when we are disconnected, we sometimes seek that feeling of aliveness through drama, which can be seen as a cheap substitute. In addition, crisis and drama keep us busy and distracted from facing our emptiness and lack of connection. Drama also serves the ego by attracting attention, and sometimes sympathy, from others.

8. *The Media* tends to focus on and sensationalize problems. Ironically, a good "news day" is one in which something devastating or shocking has occurred. Our nervous systems were not designed to process all the tragedies of the world in one sitting. It's not realistic, and it puts us in an exaggerated state of fear and vulnerability that cuts us off from our true guidance.

9. *An undisciplined mind.* While we are all at different stages of the journey, and while nobody's perfect, indulging ourselves in a habitual pattern of negativity and complaining is not unlike indulging ourselves in a regular diet of chips, soda, and candy. It's obviously not good for us and demonstrates a lack of understanding (and for many of us a fundamental lack of discipline). You may have heard the saying, "I can't afford the luxury of a negative thought." This is humorous because we all know how much the ego *enjoys* negativity and complaining. Following our higher guidance requires that we do the *work* of redirecting the mind.

10. *Focusing on the past and future.* As previously discussed, spirit lives in the present moment, and so does our higher guidance. When we stop thinking and doing and start *being* in this moment, the flow of guidance is able to open up.

11. *Ignorance and resistance.* When we do not understand the laws of the universe, we tend to respond with resistance. We tense up and passively fight those things that we would do better to either accept or work productively to change.

12. *Unconscious programming* such as "I don't deserve..." or "Life is difficult" makes up a large part of the human mind and can undermine and sabotage our efforts to be in the flow of our highest guidance. Psychoanalysis and other therapies arose from the idea that making the unconscious *conscious,* and then working through that material, would release us from the bondage of the lower mind.

13. *Inability to forgive* not only can cause lifelong suffering, illness, and violence, but represents the rejection of spiritual guidance in favor of the ego's world of duality and separation. Forgiveness reconnects us to spirit.

You Don't Have to Go It Alone

As a therapist trained in the field of counseling psychology, I am all too aware of the history of sincere, yet nonproductive and sometimes even harmful, modalities and techniques that have been used in the name of self-discovery. It brings to mind the experimental drugs and procedures performed on people and lab animals. I think it's fair to say that over the last several decades there have been many breakthroughs and many failures.

While much of the above is still going on, we now have the benefit of both years of trial and error and the natural process of evolution. For instance, in the last ten years, I have noticed a shift in the counseling world from more traditional, psychological approaches to what I would call softer, more spiritually compatible approaches. Since the early nineties, I've been receiving announcements for therapy-related workshops and seminars. I used to just throw them away because I had lost faith in psychology as an effective path to healing, but in the last few years, I've been seeing more and more integrative approaches, such as Sufi psychology, Buddhist-oriented therapy, and therapist workshops based on applying spiritual laws, utilizing gratitude, or teaching forgiveness. These are becoming popular, mainstream practices.

We now have access to many wise and sophisticated teachers, therapists, energy workers, healers, spiritual practitioners, support groups, meditation groups, metaphysical tools, rehab programs, books, films, Web sites, etc., that can *assist* us in refining our relationships with ourselves. These resources can help us get unstuck, support us when we're down, and educate us on how to tap into our intuition, but they can never replace our higher guidance, which is our own personal beacon of divine light.

PART II

Remembering
Spiritual Law

REMEMBERING SPIRITUAL LAW

As spiritual beings, eternal souls who have been on this path for eons, we are intimately familiar with the laws of the universe. Most of us, however, have forgotten these truths in the memory-erasing process of reincarnation, as well as in the mental reprogramming that occurs in our current cultural, religious, and family-based belief systems.

Right now, your Higher Self has full access to everything you've ever learned or experienced in your lengthy and distinguished soul history. Deep in your heart, you know the secrets of the universe—perhaps not fully, but the more mature and experienced your soul, the more you ultimately understand the workings of nature and the divine. Therefore, it is not a matter of *learning* the spiritual laws, but remembering them, reawakening that part of yourself that already holds the keys to the kingdom. Not only does this serve to reconnect you more fully with your Higher Self, but it helps you see where your present-life conditioning has led you astray.

Understanding the spiritual laws is like understanding the customs and laws of the land. For instance, if you know that making a U-turn might get you in trouble or cause an accident, you can consciously choose whether or not to do that. Likewise, if you know that your thoughts create your experiences, you can decide whether or not you want to put energy into changing your thoughts. It's as simple as that.

There are many, many spiritual laws—some of which are more relevant to our awakening process than others. Spiritual laws govern the patterns and structures of nature and existence, from the smallest particles to the largest galaxies, and from the outer physical world to the inner personal world of our psyches. If applied effectively, the same laws that direct nature can direct our own awesome powers of manifestation.

These laws operate regardless of whether we believe in them or not, so whether we see them as primarily spiritual or scientifically mechanistic in nature, they hold the power to change our lives. The following is an overview of the ideas and the laws that I have found to be most valuable in the process of spiritual awakening.

SEVEN

The Law of Attraction

In essence, the law of attraction says that *like attracts like.* You may or may not already be intimately familiar with this law, but let's first take a moment to put it in context. For our purposes, it could be said that the law of attraction is the fundamental operating system of our universe. In Deepak Chopra's book, *The Seven Spiritual Laws of Success*, the law of attraction is not listed as *one* of the seven spiritual laws, per se, because the law of attraction basically includes these seven as sublaws. For instance, the law of *karma* focuses on accountability for one's behavior and is based on the principle that like attracts like. Correspondingly, the law of *circulation* says that what you give you will receive.

The law of attraction teaches that our every thought, feeling, word, and action create our life experiences and that there is no randomness or chance involved in this whatsoever. You may be wondering, "How could that be so? How could I have created my early childhood experiences?" We will look at that

85

in depth later, but for now, suffice it to say that every single experience in your soul's history has led you to this lifetime and that every thought has led you to this moment in time. What's more, this is exactly where you need to be, and ultimately, it's all good.

So whatever we put our attention on expands or increases, while what we withhold our attention from decreases. The law doesn't distinguish between what we want and what we don't want, nor does it distinguish between what is good and what is not good. In other words, you might want a great relationship, but the fact is that your thoughts are centered around the reality that you don't have a relationship. In effect, the universe hears, "no relationship," and delivers that.

In reality, the universe doesn't hear your words or read your thoughts at all, but rather interprets your *vibration,* which is based on how you feel. You needn't worry so much about the exact wording of your affirmations, but rather how they make you *feel* when you think them or state them. You might be saying, "I'm ready for a great relationship. God, please send me the perfect mate," but your vibration is tinged with sadness and an underlying doubt that a perfect mate even exists. The universe still reads this signal as "no relationship, *yet.*"

On the other hand, someone who is ready, willing, and able to see himself in a great relationship feels excited and puts out a strong, affirmative signal. The universe then sends someone who is a vibrational *match* to that signal. Now, if this person had put out a lower-frequency signal, like, "I'm definitely ready, willing, and able to have a *mediocre* relationship," then that's exactly what he'd attract. It's not as important what you say as how you feel and the quality of the vibration you're transmitting.

Another example would be *complementary* vibrations. Let's say that you know a lovely, kind woman who always seems to get involved with abusive men. How can it be true that like attracts like? The relationship signal she may be putting out is, "I want to be with a nice man, but the guys I attract always push me around," or "My father was abusive. My first husband was abusive. That's just how men are." She may even seek out a passive, soft-spoken man only to find out later that he has a terrible temper.

Now let's look at her would-be suitor. The relationship signal he's putting out is, "I want a lovely, kind lady who knows her place. Women are like children—they need to be disciplined."

You can see how these two have attracted each other. In terms of relationship, they are a vibrational match. However, if one evolves to a higher vibration, they will no longer be compatible. Our job as spiritual seekers is to become compatible with that which we desire, whatever that may be.

As human beings, we each have thousands of thoughts every day, but most of these thoughts are the same ones, day in and day out. If you examine yourself objectively, you'll notice a habitual pattern in your thinking, which is unique to you. This may be more easily seen in your friends and family members. You might not know exactly what they are thinking, but you can predict how they will respond to a given situation, and you can see that their thoughts and beliefs have a particular "signature." Even though you don't have access to their soul history or to the inner workings of their minds, you can understand why their lives are the way they are.

For instance, my sister is a positive, successful woman. She makes thoughtful decisions, is emotionally balanced, and has loving relationships. Even though I don't have access to her inner thoughts or records of past lives, I can see clearly that the success and harmony she manifests in her life is an exact match to the vibration she is putting out to the universe.

Conversely, another woman I know could be called a "drama queen." She always seems to be in one crisis or another, be it a car accident, being bitten by a dog, getting involved with a sex addict, being framed for possession of illegal drugs, losing her life savings, the list goes on. People have said, "How can she be so unlucky? Everything happens to that poor woman!"

Of course, luck has nothing to do with it. For whatever reason, her chaotic thinking pattern and poor life choices have created all of these situations. Maybe she's an adrenaline addict; maybe she's afraid that if things calmed down she would have to face her emptiness; or maybe she contracted to have these experiences for some karmic purpose. Whatever the reason, the vibration she puts out to the universe keeps a steady stream of crises flowing her way.

Managing the Ego's Attraction to the Law

From a spiritual point of view, the law of attraction is neutral. From a spiritual *seeker* point of view, working with the law of attraction can be satisfying as well as challenging. This is due to the manifestation focus we apply to it. The law of attraction says you can have anything you want as long as you are a vibrational match to it. You can have unlimited wealth, love, happiness. You can have the perfect relationship, the perfect job, perfect health, etc. Well, that all sounds wonderful, especially to the ego or lower self. Herein lies the potential problem.

As human beings we want to be happy, healthy, and have all of our physical needs met. We look around us and see infinite possibilities for achieving these objectives. We see beautiful clothes, cars, and homes. We see people who have great jobs, great partners, and lots of free time. If you have good self-esteem, you probably want the best for yourself, whatever this means to you personally. For instance, if you are a visually oriented person, it will mean something different than if you are a feeling-oriented person. One might want to be surrounded by people, places, and objects that express the beauty in life, whereas the other desires most to be comfortable and feel loved.

The challenge occurs when our egos realize that we can have anything we want by successfully applying manifestation *techniques*, such as visualization, affirmations, etc. The ego loves to acquire and achieve. The ego loves to compare and contrast. The ego would have us believe that our emptiness can be filled by material objects, worldly success, relationships, food, drugs, etc. In fact, to a large degree, the ego's survival depends on us *not* awakening and remembering that we are already whole and divine.

Applying law of attraction-based techniques, if we are not careful, can actually have the effect of putting our egos in charge of creating our futures, and you may have noticed that this is what got us into trouble in the first place. Our ultimate success lies in putting our Higher Selves in charge of our lives. Our Higher Selves want what is best for us. Sometimes this includes fame and fortune, and sometimes it does not.

A few years ago when the film *The Secret* became popular, there was criticism from the spiritual community that the film focused too much attention on material manifestation. While I agreed to some extent, I was delighted nonetheless to see that the general population had embraced the principles of the law of attraction. In fact, I thought it ingenious that the producers had managed to ride that line between creating a spiritual piece and creating something that would appeal so greatly to the American ego.

Even if many people considered it a get-rich-quick scheme, I sensed that they would eventually land where we all do, which is to say that once you realize you create (or prevent) your own success, it's just a matter of time before you realize you are creating *everything*. Once this happens, you're well over halfway home.

So vibration attracts like vibration. Thoughts create after their own kind. Feelings draw to us that which would have us continue to feel the same way. Beliefs create our future. Actions produce karma, pleasant or not so pleasant. You can see how objective this all is. The universe is not deciding who deserves what, but rather *we* are transmitting to the universe what we believe we deserve, or at least what we believe is real.

EIGHT

The Law of Unity

The law of unity is the basis for all that exists. Every being, every thought, every place, every object is part of source energy, and we are all connected within a field of the same energy. Your Higher Self is pure consciousness, as is true of every being. We are all one flame, all sparks of the divine. The idea that we are separate is purely a construct of the ego, a thought set into motion so that we could experience duality for the purpose of spiritual expansion. Newtonian physics anchored this belief in for centuries, and it still lingers in our consciousness today.

The field of pure potentiality goes by many names. For centuries people have referred to it as the "ether," the Buddhist Sutras call it the "net," the Hopi tradition calls it the "web," the Vedas call it a unified field of "pure consciousness," Abraham-Hicks calls it the "vortex," and Gregg Braden calls it the "divine matrix." Even modern physics agrees that there exists a "quantum field" of energy that connects all aspects of creation, from thinker to thought to manifestation.

Regardless of the name, the idea is the same: there is no empty space; everything is part of the fabric of creation. The field is made up of pure energy and information.

In his book *The Divine Matrix*, Gregg Braden (former senior aerospace computer systems designer) explains the origin of the universe. Apparently between thirteen and twenty billion years ago, just before the big bang, our universe was the size of a green pea, and the temperature within that tiny space was an unfathomable eighteen billion million million million degrees! As it exploded into the existing emptiness, it set forth a pattern of energy, or blueprint, for all that would ever be. It created the field of pure potentiality, or what he calls the divine matrix.

Braden goes on to say, "The fact that the protons and the particles from the big bang were once physically part of one another is the key to their connectivity. It appears that once something is joined, *it is always connected,* whether it remains physically linked or not."[1] Thus, everything in existence is connected within this great net, web, or matrix, and all we have to do to tap into this powerful field is to view ourselves as *part of* the universe and not a *separate* entity.

Once we realize that we are all connected, all brothers and sisters with each other, with the plants and animals, with Mother Earth, and with the rest of the universe, then life becomes truly magical. At first this can be humbling, though, because we have to take responsibility for our feelings and interactions on a higher level.

For example, let's say you have a prejudice. Perhaps you've always disliked lawyers. You may or may not be aware of why you feel this way; all you know is that you don't trust them and you question their integrity. In the world of the ego, where we're separate, you can always find others who agree with you, and you can find documented evidence to support the way you feel.

However, in the world of spirit and within the divine network, we're all one. You and the lawyer are parts of the same whole. You are different expressions of the same *One*, and the fact that you dislike your neighbor can mean only that you dislike a part of yourself.

We've all known people who are critical or intolerant of others. We tend to want to think that they are satisfied with themselves while being dissatisfied with other people. This is almost never the case. The judgmental person is most likely extremely judgmental toward himself, even if he would never admit it. This is a form of self-projection, and we humans do it all the time. Not only do we do this when we don't like something about ourselves, we also do it when we meet someone who displays a part of ourselves that we might love, but is perhaps hidden within us.

The obvious example of this is when you are attracted to someone or something. When you are drawn to another person, be it sexual or platonic, you are seeing something in that person that you wouldn't be able to see if it didn't already exist within yourself. When you have a crush on a particular actor or singer, for instance, consider what it is that she is reflecting to you about yourself. Maybe you feel that she "gets" you, that her songs or roles touch you deeply or make you feel more alive. In this example, the attraction is probably not based on karmic ties or a soul mate relationship, as sometimes attraction can be, but rather on your relationship with self. The artist evokes in you something that you were out of touch with until she expressed it. You might feel that she is the source of that experience, but in fact, it was dormant within you all along.

The world is very much our mirror. Whatever we see or notice in our world is a reflection of what we see inside ourselves, whether we're aware of that aspect or not. A friend of mine once said, "I'm a realist. I'm not going to pretend that the world is a lovely place when I can see otherwise." The truth is that we're *all* realists. We all look upon the world and see what we believe is real, and then we make it so, time and time again. There are as many "realities" as there are beings in the universe. The good news is that if you don't like what you see in your world, you can change it by tapping into the law of unity, or pure potentiality.

Being One with the Law of Unity

How do you do this? First of all recognize that you are part of everything that has ever existed, good and "bad" alike. Any judgment you have about yourself or others is nothing more than the ego perceiving itself as separate. Judgment (as opposed to discernment, which is extremely valuable) causes a constant stream of interference between yourself and source energy. When you stop evaluating and labeling everything, even for a moment, your mind naturally relaxes and opens to the expansive field of pure potentiality. As often as possible, go to your heart, and practice the art of nonjudgment.

Next, practice consciously tapping into this field by quieting your mind and simply being. Most spiritual teachers recommend a daily practice of meditation. While this is excellent advice, many earnest spiritual seekers have difficulty actually doing this. There are a thousand reasons why we don't set aside time for meditation even when we are fully aware of its benefits.

If this is your experience, it might be helpful to get in touch with what the resistance is about. Becoming proficient at meditation can require patience and practice, so be prepared to work through some awkwardness, but please don't tyrannize yourself about it. Instead acknowledge the ways that you are already quieting your mind, ways that you love and are natural to you personally, and indulge yourself in doing those things more often.

For example, I love my daily solo walk. It has the effect of getting me in touch with what's really going on for me and then releasing that energy, if necessary. In addition to its other benefits, the walking process releases tension, increases the flow of life force energy, and ultimately quiets my mind and produces a euphoric feeling. This is exactly what meditation does for us.

So if instead of sitting in meditation, you'd rather go for a silent walk, run, or bike ride, by all means do that. Or if gazing at the ocean, holding a pet, lying on a rock, or creating art helps you quiet your mind, do one of those things. Trying to force or discipline yourself to sit in meditation when you really don't want to can be counterproductive.

NINE

The Law of Circulation

The law of circulation says that we live in a universe based on dynamic exchange, or continuous giving and receiving. Everything is in a state of flux. Our physical bodies are always exchanging matter with the earth, plants, and animals, and our minds and hearts are always making energetic exchanges with other beings and within the universal matrix. Just as breathing is critical to physical survival, giving and receiving love (the *stuff* of spirit) is critical to our emotional and spiritual well-being.

You've probably known people who freely and joyfully give of themselves, whether it's their time, money, smiles, love, compliments, or whatever it may be. These folks are clearly participating in the flow of life, and being around them feels easy, comfortable, and "clean." They know on a deep level that giving *is* receiving; there's really no difference. When you are in that loop, it feels natural, it feels right, and it feels good.

In contrast, you may have known people who are guarded and withholding of their energy, whatever forms it may take, and have cut themselves off from the flow of life. Their hearts are closed, and often their disposition is one of irritability or even overt hostility. They don't trust the universe, and they believe that if they give, they will lose something. This is the stance of the ego and is based on fear and a belief in limited resources.

Personally, you've probably noticed the difference you feel when you engage in healthy habits like exercising, breathing deeply, meditating, communicating effectively, getting adequate rest, and eating nutritious foods. Energetically, these habits have the effect of maintaining the flow of life force energy (also called chi, ki, or prana) within your body and energetic field. When we're under stress, sedentary, breathing shallowly, polluting our bodies with toxins, or stuffing our feelings, the flow slows down dramatically, and we feel out of sorts.

A good example of this is common depression. Usually there are unresolved emotions buried deep within, possibly old grief, repressed anger, or any number of other feelings that have accumulated and been stowed away. Active, *alive* emotions have a different quality. For instance, extreme sadness may feel excruciating, but the very act of *feeling* it causes it to be transformed and released. The energy keeps flowing.

Conversely, repressing sadness wreaks havoc on your entire system: physical, mental, emotional, and spiritual. Not only does the system lock down, but a tremendous amount of energy is required to continue blocking unwanted feelings from surfacing. People who habitually repress their true emotions eventually end up ill, depressed, addicted, behaving violently, or exhibiting any number of other physical or psychological symptoms.

On the upside, the law of circulation says that whatever you give, you will receive. If you give love, you will receive love. If you give money, you will receive money. However, if you give anger, you will receive anger. The true vibration of what you give will yield what you receive. What does that mean, the *true vibration*?

This is a very important point. Let's say that your friend is encouraging you to tithe, that is give 10 percent of your income to your church or to another cause you support. She says that since she has been tithing she feels wonderful and has been attracting more money from the universe. She keeps receiving unexpected checks in the mail.

So you decide you're going to try tithing. Each month you submit your donation, but you feel uneasy. Even though you believe that tithing "works," you can't help but think about what you could otherwise be buying. Even though you're giving a lot of money, the fact is that your heart is not in it, and your true vibration is one of ambivalence and doubt. Your friend may be receiving checks in the mail, but you probably will not.

The same goes for anything you give. If you give a sincere, heartfelt compliment it will have a different effect than if you attempt to flatter someone. The words could be the same, and the recipient might not know the difference, but what you are actually giving will determine what flows back to you. If you give authenticity, you will receive authenticity. If you give for some other reason, as we all sometimes do, you will receive accordingly.

As a therapist, I have known many people who identify with being a helper or giver. They are constantly doing for others and often feel depleted, taken for granted, or even resentful. Perhaps they don't know how to say "no." They are clearly not getting back what they believe they have been giving. The problem, of course, is that their giving, at least some portion of it, comes from a place of lack. A person may truly love to help others and may receive great appreciation and love in return. The same person may sometimes give out of habit, obligation, neediness, or poor boundaries, and find herself exhausted and unappreciated. Often givers have an underdeveloped ability to *receive*, which means that they are not tapped into the law of circulation. They give and give, but they block receiving.

A subtle phenomenon I've noticed in myself occurs when I believe that I've given something from a place of love, without the slightest conscious thought of what I will get in return, only to end up noticing that I never received a thank you note! In many of these cases, I was unconsciously hoping to receive appreciation from the recipient, which meant that I wasn't giving as freely as I had thought. In other cases, the giving was coming from that pure place of my Higher Self, but later, in a weak moment, ego kicked in and started looking for ways to feel unappreciated, which the ego likes to do. The ego loves to keep score.

Tapping into the Law of Circulation

How do you make the most of the law of circulation? The first thing is to take a loving, but honest appraisal of yourself.

In what areas of your life are you in the flow? Do you give and receive kindness, but block the flow of money? Do you give in order to receive love or validation? Do you take from others without giving care and respect? Are you generally guarded and blocked? This may be difficult to look at, especially if you've been working on yourself for years and doing your best to be a good person, but it's worth it. Once you make the necessary adjustments and get in the *big* flow, everything gets easier, and manifesting what you desire becomes natural. This brings us to our next law, the law of nonresistance.

TEN

The Law of Nonresistance

Nature has so much to teach us. All we have to do is observe the perfectly orchestrated change of seasons to see that Mother Nature has her own intelligence. Trees don't try to grow; they just grow. Animals don't need parenting books; they instinctively know how to carry, give birth, and raise their young. Bees pollinate flowers because that's their job. Nature knows how to go with the flow, and nature accepts the facts of life: beauty, birth, creation, gorgeous sunsets, survival of the fittest, violence, death, devastating fires, floods, and earthquakes. There's an amazing ability and necessity within nature to accept life on life's terms.

On the other hand, while there are plenty of exceptions, the developed world has a difficult time accepting the most basic givens of life, and we expend a huge amount of precious energy resisting those very conditions. You can probably think of dozens of ways that we repress and fight nature.

Especially in the United States, we have a tendency to form an opinion about the way something *should* be and then fight like hell to make it so.

For instance, as a culture we've decided that normal aging is unacceptable, so we take pills, buy expensive creams, exercise compulsively, undergo plastic surgery, dye our hair, etc. Anything to look younger (or thinner), because the consensus is that aging is a terrible fate. Likewise, dying a natural death, even at a ripe old age, has become unusual because doctors are trained to keep people alive at all costs.

Conversely, Buddhism and many other traditions *embrace* the facts of human life. To a large extent, acceptance of what *is* forms the cornerstone of the relationship with life, the world, and all that exists. When we accept that loss is a part of life, it is a different experience than when we resist the loss. Either way, we may be grief stricken when a loved one dies, but when we're grounded in the fact that physical death is natural and inevitable, we suffer much less than when our grief is complicated by the belief that something has gone terribly wrong.

Recently I saw a news report about a college student who had died of a congenital disease. His friends all knew about his serious condition, but when he passed away, they were in a state of absolute disbelief, and they all said the same thing, "Nineteen-year-olds are not supposed to die!" The sad truth, however, is that every year millions and millions of nineteen-year-olds die.

The same is true for infant mortality, less so in the United States today, but in other parts of the world it is as prevalent as ever. In the early 1900s when my Grandmother Beulah was a child, her mother birthed fifteen babies, five of whom died.

Equally distressing was that when Beulah was very young her father disappeared mysteriously one day, and was presumed to be dead. Out in the country where her family lived, things like that just happened.

In *those* days, people were clear about the human condition, and while that kind of grief and loss can be heartbreaking, it also teaches us that birth and death, joy and sorrow, good times and hard times are normal and natural, and it is up to us how we let those experiences affect us. Beulah became so strong and robust that she lived to be 102.

When you realize and *accept* that you could lose everything you have in the physical world tomorrow, you gain a freedom and a strength that you didn't have before. When you really understand that you're a spiritual being having a human experience, you start to release the death grip you have on worldly life. When you realize that the relationships you have with loved ones never really end, but keep changing and growing stronger throughout eternity, you become less dependent on those people and more truly loving of them. I believe that nothing worth having can ever be truly lost to us.

There are a multitude of ways in which we resist feeling our emotions, and feeling our emotions is critical to our overall health and well-being. The problem with expressing our feelings is that this often makes other people uncomfortable. It starts with the crying baby, who is doing the healthy thing by expressing his discomfort or dissatisfaction. If we parents were able to simply *respond* to the crying, all would be well, but the fact is that most of us can't tolerate the crying, so we do *anything* to make it stop. And the pattern is established.

Very few parents are able to sit down with their misbehaving child and say, "Wow, you're really upset. How about telling me what's bothering you." If we were able to do this for our children, they would learn that their feelings are normal and acceptable, and they wouldn't need to *stuff* them. They would identify a feeling, address it, and then release it.

The law of nonresistance says that there is a divine, natural order in the universe, and that ultimately everything is as it should be *in this moment*. That doesn't mean that the unspeakable things that occur in our world are divinely sanctioned, but that even in the fray, there is meaning and purpose. There's nothing to fight, per se, because being in the flow means accepting what *is*, and then, if necessary, working on a solution. This is what Mother Teresa modeled. When asked to attend an anti-war rally, she declined, but added that if there was to be a *peace* rally, she would gladly attend.

In the law of attraction books by Esther and Jerry Hicks, Abraham uses the analogy of a rowboat in the river. We are the boats, and when we take our oars out of the water and go with the natural flow of the river, we are taken "downstream" to our highest good. Everything we really want exists downstream. Our ego is inclined to fight the current and try to control where the boat goes. In fact, more often than not, the ego puts the oars in the water and tries to paddle "upstream."[1]

This, of course, is exhausting, nonproductive, and takes us somewhere other than where we truly want to be. We may achieve some level of success this way, but not the true success we would enjoy had we gone with the natural flow of our higher good.

The ego would have us believe that getting what you want requires 5 percent inspiration and 95 percent perspiration. Spirit has it the other way around. When you're tapped into the field of pure potentiality, everything is relatively easy, and much less effort is required on your part. When you're in the flow of your highest good, you're doing what you came here to do, and you're joyful; therefore, the actions required to realize your goal will not even feel like work. If you're not enjoying your work, you're probably paddling upstream, and the end result most likely will not be as satisfying as you had hoped. Even if you succeed in making a lot of money, you may end up feeling empty or unfulfilled.

The better you get at going with the flow of your highest good—which means letting spirit run your life instead of the ego—the easier it becomes to achieve everything that you actually want. I say *actually want* because what your ego wants and what your Higher Self wants may be different. The ego tends to want status, control over others, possessions, and whatever provides pleasure right now. The Higher Self, on the other hand, wants what would bring you the truest satisfaction, which probably includes loving relationships, rewarding work, physical comfort and vitality, etc. It may or may not include great financial success.

Only your spirit knows what will bring you joy, and joy is the key. When you are tapped into this carefree state, which is really the opposite of resistance, you can manifest anything with the faintest of thoughts, because joy is the language of spirit. When we communicate joy, mountains will move for us. However, when we go back to resistance, the magic comes to a screeching halt. Relatively speaking, the power of the ego pulls little weight.

Going with the Flow of Nonresistance

How do we put the law of nonresistance into action? The first step is to face the realities of the human condition. The painful truth is that we live in an imperfect world, a world where we learn through trial and error, and sometimes through great suffering and loss. Accepting this basic premise actually frees up a lot of energy that can be used for creating more of what you *do* want.

Acceptance as a spiritual practice is a beautiful thing. It is the sister of forgiveness, and like forgiveness, it disengages the ego and connects us with our higher spiritual self. Instead of indulging the ego in faultfinding and resisting life, say "yes" to life by doing your best to accept everything the way it is *in this moment*. It doesn't mean you don't wish for a better future scenario or that you needn't work for change. It means only that in this moment you accept everything and everybody the way they are. This may not be easy, but it may also not be as difficult as you think. Give it a try, and you will learn a lot about yourself.

Remember, too, that you are one of the heroes of the universe. You volunteered to come here knowing it would be full of trials and tribulations, illusions of weakness, failure, and death. But you came anyway, because you *knew* you could do this, and you knew your service here would benefit all life throughout creation.

Next, begin to challenge the puritan belief that says you have to work hard and struggle to get what you want or need. That is the "upstream" thinking of the ego. When your boat is floating effortlessly downstream, your life will not feel like struggle. It will feel invigorating and satisfying, and you'll be guided to take the right actions at the right time to manifest the highest good. Perspiration is optional.

Finally, try to adopt a stance of nondefensiveness. The bigger your ego, the more energy you are likely to put into validating and defending yourself and persuading others that your ideas are right. What if you didn't feel the need to prove anything? When we are operating from spirit, we see that everyone is entitled to his own opinion and that the way other people see us is ultimately their own business. When you stop worrying about what other people think, you free up a great deal of life force energy that can be harnessed for your own and everyone else's higher good.

ELEVEN

The Law of Karma

The law of karma, or *cause and effect*, is one of the most misunderstood of the universal laws. This is due to our ego's orientation toward duality: right and wrong, innocence and guilt, victim and perpetrator. Through the eyes of the ego (and society), if we do something "bad," we expect to be punished; whereas if we do something "good," we expect to be rewarded.

From the perspective of spirit, it is not so black and white. Unlike the physical world, in the spirit world there's really nobody outside of ourselves judging us or deciding what price we're going to pay for our misdeeds. Ultimately, we are our only judges. Rather than punishment, the point of karma is to balance that which is out of balance. In fact, it could be argued that our primary purpose for being here in this polarity game is to achieve soul balance. If we can find equilibrium here in the midst of emotional chaos and drama, then we have learned our lessons on a deep level indeed.

Like the law of attraction, the law of karma says that every word and deed acts like a boomerang. Whatever we throw out there will eventually come back to us. It might not look the same, but the lesson or the vibrational content will match. It may come back to us instantaneously, like the guilt we feel when we've hurt someone's feelings, or it may take lifetimes to manifest, but manifest it will.

The important thing to realize is that the process of karma is ultimately our friend. The fact that we are sensitive, spiritually aware people *now* is the result of all the pain and suffering we've experienced and caused in the past. The great Yogananda was quoted to have said, "A saint is a sinner who never gave up."

Just maybe all those "bad guys" out there are representative of ourselves a few lifetimes ago. One of the reasons we might choose not to kill, steal from others, or commit adultery in this lifetime is that we've already done these things in previous incarnations and found out the hard way what it feels like to either experience deep remorse or to have these acts done unto us.

Our souls learn through trial and error (just as children do) what works for us and what doesn't. Cause and effect says that if a little boy sticks his hand in the fire he's going to get burned. This is how he learns. There's no judgment or punishment attached. Firsthand experience is simply the most effective means we have had on earth for learning.

So if we're saying that whatever we put out there comes back to us in the form of karma, positive or negative, does that mean that nothing comes to us that we have not in some way created? The law of cause and effect says yes, in one way or another, we have created or attracted every experience in our lives, *especially* the life-changing ones. There are no random accidents, and sometimes we set up contracts to experience great difficulty or even death for a particular reason or purpose.

When you have a loving thought, you attract love from the universe. When you harm another, you create a karmic debt that you will eventually *want* to repay, because as sparks of the divine we seek love and balance. If you are consciously aware, you will register the misdeed and set out to repair it, but if you are unwilling or unable to do so in your current lifetime, you will have to face this debt once you have left the physical body.

What does this mean exactly? Dr. Michael Newton, creator of the therapy model *Life between Lives Hypnotherapy*, explains the typical life review process described by many of the over seven thousand hypnotherapy clients he has served during his forty-year career.[1]

According to Newton's clients, following an incarnation, we meet with a council of elders to discuss and review our behavior and actions during the lifetime we just completed. At this meeting, it becomes obvious to us what mistakes we have made, especially if we have harmed others, and we begin to consider how we might rectify these misdeeds in future incarnations. The council is there for our growth and benefit, and they are understanding of our human weaknesses. Their purpose is to guide and direct, not to judge or apply punishment.

A second meeting may occur when we are planning our next incarnation, to evaluate potential life choices and opportunities to balance karma. For instance, if we abused children in our previous incarnation, we may choose to be born into an abusive family. This way we learn on an experiential level the effect of our prior behavior. Otherwise, upon reincarnating, we would likely pick up where we left off and repeat our old patterns. The law of karma helps us to get back on track, so that we may continue making progress on our spiritual path, through physical incarnations and beyond. When seen from a larger perspective, it is a blessing, not a curse.

In discussions of karmic accountability, I have often heard people present arguments like, "What about the innocent baby? What could she have done to deserve *this*?" What must be understood is that the innocent baby is actually an experienced soul, just like you, who made conscious agreements with other souls before incarnating into her present lifetime.

She may seem vulnerable, and from a human perspective she is, but from a higher spiritual perspective, she knows exactly what she has signed up for and is not really a victim. No matter what the issue: illness, violence, etc., her soul has agreed to this life experience for the purpose of her own and/or another's spiritual growth.

Of course, this doesn't mean we should ignore or be insensitive to the pain of others; suffering is suffering, after all. In fact, it may be our purpose to alleviate the pain of others, but we must avoid getting caught up in the black-and-white thinking of the ego.

One of my all-time favorite quotes is from the book *Illusions*, by Richard Bach. He wrote, "The mark of your ignorance is the depth of your belief in injustice and tragedy. What a caterpillar calls the end of the world the master calls a butterfly."[2] Many people find this quote disconcerting, as it forces them to confront their deepest-held beliefs about human life, but others find it a breath of fresh air.

Spirit would tell us that in the broader scheme every event in our lives is there to support our highest good and the highest good of all involved. Remembering who we are means seeing ourselves and everyone else as ultimately whole and well, regardless of appearances.

Some might argue, "That's easy for you to say. You're not living in poverty. You haven't lost a child. Sometimes life is unfair." This may be true, but keep in mind that this perspective is based on the notion that we only get one shot at life or that the fate we have in one lifetime is somehow reflective of our soul's permanent fate, and therefore, some people are blessed while others are cursed. If this were the case, then life would indeed be hideously unfair. However, if we have hundreds or thousands of lifetimes, and each one is a mere drop in the bucket to our eternal soul, then one lifetime of great strife may be what we have consciously contracted for to make significant progress on our spiritual path.

Sometimes a soul chooses an accelerated path or lifetime, which includes painful and dramatic lessons, whereas other times the soul may choose a more moderate path or lifetime, which includes subtler lessons. He may even choose an easy or uneventful lifetime, one that is designed to be restorative or emotionally corrective.

As a therapist, one thing I've learned is that it's useless to judge another person's suffering. In fact, we can't even estimate the extent of another person's suffering (or lack thereof) because we don't have access to his soul's history. For example, a person might be experiencing what looks like an easy lifetime. He has money, a nice place to live, good physical health, and loving friends, but he is so tormented by his unresolved past-life traumas that getting out of bed is a struggle for him. Add to the torment that he has no idea why he feels this way. He sees that there are starving people in the world, and he feels even worse about himself because he doesn't have any "real" problems. He may become suicidal, and no one, including himself, understands why.

Conversely, another person may find herself in an extremely undesirable lifetime. She may be poverty-stricken, living in a war zone, and pregnant, but inexplicably she possesses peace of mind. On some deep, perhaps unconscious level she knows she is in the perfect place, experiencing what she needs to experience for her ultimate spiritual good and the good of others. This brings up an important issue: the overall good.

You may still be wondering how an event that kills hundreds, thousands, or even millions of people fits into this karma scheme. This is an extremely big question and one I don't pretend to be able to answer well, but here are a couple ideas to consider for yourself.

First of all, let's take a deep breath and remember who we are. If we are eternal, divine beings who are here to learn and grow spiritually, then no real harm can come to us, and no lasting harm has *ever* come to us, or anyone else. I believe that this is how God sees us. It is not that God is insensitive to our suffering, but rather that he/she does not experience the illusion that we could be harmed. God knows the truth of who we are, even if we have temporarily forgotten.

Secondly, as inconceivable as it may seem, what if such devastating events were somehow purposeful? Let's take a simple example from nature. Fire is a natural part of life in the forest. While we think of forest fires as something to be avoided at all costs, that is not the way of nature. Some trees actually depend on fire in order to propagate, and an extended period without fire can wreak havoc on the forest.

Similar examples can be found throughout nature and throughout human history. We may not appreciate that 3-D life sometimes needs to destroy to make room for something new, but this is the case. Sometimes plants, animals, people, and even large groups of people consent to forego their physical bodies for some greater, unexplained purpose. The elderly pass away to make room for incoming babies.

The ego wants to judge every person and every situation it encounters, but what if the *mystery* is so rich and multidimensional that we can never understand it with our human minds? Perhaps then we would learn to turn all questions and concerns over to our Higher Selves. This is an important part of what the processes of spiritual awakening and establishing inner peace are all about.

Putting Karma to Rest

While the law of karma has been an important part of our overall operating system for eons, there is a growing belief that the karma game has played itself out and that we are entering a new age where it will no longer be necessary.

Whether this is something that is occurring now or will occur in some future Utopia is hard to say, but it does appear that the nature of our karmic world is changing and that many people are instinctively processing and burning karma at an accelerated rate.

Kryon explains that only recently has it become possible for humans to eliminate or sidestep the karma we were born with. They claim that by becoming spiritually conscious, we can now *decide* to cancel our birth karma and consciously forge new paths for ourselves that aren't based on the past. When this process has been successfully negotiated, we may find ourselves strangely free of the phobias, grudges, etc., that had previously held us hostage.[3] The trick is to release the now-empty karmic "container" so that it does not fill up again purely out of habit.

The following are a few ideas for wrapping up any remaining karmic debts you may have. I like to say that intention is nine-tenths of the law, meaning that in this energy-based universe, we can sometimes transform and heal by applying our loving intentions alone. We can release or transmute our karma (change negative energy into pure, positive energy) by being present with our current experiences and asking ourselves if there's anything left to be learned from them. If the lesson is complete, we should be able to consciously release the karma, through our focused intention, and move on.

Another option is to attempt to transcend or burn away any remaining karma through meditation and visualization practices, or energy work like Reiki. In essence, we are asking our guides to work with us to bypass the experiences of negative karma that we no longer feel are necessary for our spiritual growth. Of course, our guides know whether or not we still need to walk through these karmic experiences, as sometimes we do; nonetheless, I have found that asking for their help is always beneficial, even if they are not able to deliver the specific help I am asking for.

There are also CDs, workshops, etc., available today that focus on releasing past karma. These resources are most valuable when applied side by side with your highest intention to stay conscious of your words and actions and to live at the highest possible level of integrity.

TWELVE

The Laws of Intention
And Detachment

As previously discussed, we live in an energetic field of pure consciousness, which goes by many names: ether, the quantum field, the net, the web, the divine matrix, etc. We are aware that within this field *like attracts like*, but how does this work? How does the universe actually deliver to us what we hold in our minds? Physician and spiritual teacher Deepak Chopra provides the following explanation.[1]

The quantum field, and everything in it, is made up of *energy* and *information*, and is influenced by desire and *intention*. Physically, the human, plant, and animal life-forms on earth are made up of basically the same recycled elements: mostly carbon, hydrogen, oxygen, and nitrogen, and we are constantly exchanging these elements with each other. What truly distinguishes us from one another, at this level, is differences in the energy and information content of our bodies and minds.

The beauty and the curse of being human is that we have complex nervous systems that allow us to be *consciously aware* of our own thoughts, emotions, desires, memories, drives, beliefs, etc. There is no separation between our bodies (our personal quantum fields) and the rest of the universe (the larger quantum field). Through intention and what we give attention to, we are accessing that greater field and effectively commanding it to conform to our deepest held beliefs. We do this without even realizing it. Our thoughts, feelings, and beliefs have the power to change the information and energy in our bodies, which affects or changes our extended body: the material world.

This change is made possible by two characteristics of consciousness, attention and intention. Attention activates or *energizes*, and intention triggers *transformation*, the transformation of information and energy. According to Dr. Chopra, "The quality of *intention* on the object of *attention* will orchestrate an infinity of space-time events to bring about the outcome intended, provided one follows the other spiritual laws...Intention lays the groundwork for the effortless, spontaneous, frictionless flow of pure potentiality seeking expression from the unmanifest to the manifest."[2]

Desire by itself is weak. Wanting something usually implies attachment to the outcome and does not pack the punch of true intention. Intention is desire that is tapped into the other spiritual laws, especially the law of detachment. Intention, even for the future, occurs in the present moment, which is where the power of manifestation lies. Focused, unwavering, single-pointed intention, especially for the higher good, can move mountains and part seas. This is how Jesus healed the sick, and like Jesus said, *we* can do this and more. We just need to learn how to harness the awesome power of the law of intention.

The *law of detachment* says that to manifest anything we desire in the physical universe we must surrender our attachment to it. I personally experienced this most fully when, after years and years of anxiously awaiting the arrival of my soul mate, I came to realize that I was quite content to be on my own. Within three months, my future husband appeared at my door. You may have noticed this phenomenon in your own life. You release your attachment to something, *anything*, and the situation improves almost instantly.

If, however, you just pretend to release your attachment to something, it will not have the same effect. For instance, getting upset and telling yourself or others that you "just don't care anymore" is different than releasing attachment. Likewise, playing "hard to get," giving someone the "cold shoulder," or engaging in other distancing games actually implies attachment to outcome. These tactics may have the initial effect of getting someone's attention, but that person will probably lose interest once she realizes she is being manipulated.

So what do we mean by attachment? Attachment is a function of the ego, or false self. In fact, attachment is the ego's middle name because this false self is based on the fearful belief that we are independent entities who must fend for ourselves in a 3-D world of other competing entities. Our survival depends upon getting *and keeping* what we need, be it food, money, security, or "love." We have learned, through multiple earthly incarnations, that there is feast and there is famine. We have to salt our pork for the winter and then guard it from thieves, because otherwise we will starve to death. From the ego's point of view, this is quite real.

From the perspective of the Higher Self, everything we need or could ever desire is available through our connection with spirit. It is only our thoughts and feelings of lack that produce lack in our lives. When we are tapped into the field of pure potentiality, we naturally attract abundance on every level, and even when we inevitably experience loss, as of a loved one, we see it differently. We know that everything is purposeful. This is a very different experience than going into a tailspin and clinging even more tightly to that which we think will give us security.

The irony is that there is no security in the ego's world and abundant security in the world of spirit. Nothing worth keeping can ever be lost, but can only appear to be lost. Our real work is learning to see beyond the illusions of the material world.

Attachment is always to what is known, which is based on our past, and therefore edges out the magic and mystery of the divine unknown. When we state our true desire and intention, when we know that that intention is viable, and then we release our attachment to *how* it will come to us, we enter the zone of the greatest manifesting power. The ego's frail attempts to manifest what it thinks we need do not hold a candle to the awesome forces of the universe that are available for orchestrating our highest good.

Many years ago, I was working for a company that was undergoing layoffs. In a staff meeting one morning, our boss presented a quote, which read, "The only security in life lies in relishing the insecurities of life." I will never forget that moment because, although silently, the emotion in that room went through the roof. One moment we were calmly enjoying our morning cup of coffee, and the next moment we were desperately attempting to relish the insecurities of life! Even though I didn't want to lose my job, I loved the quote because of its wisdom and truth, and I sensed that everyone in the room would be fine, no matter what became of his or her job title.

In the world of the ego, illusions of security are just that, *illusions*. The ego knows that physical death is inevitable, and therefore it lives in constant fear of annihilation. This fear is justified, because the ego does usually fade away with the body's death (although extreme attachment to the ego can sometimes cause it to remain intact after death, which slows down the soul's progression to the next level).

Conversely, in the world of spirit, there is no death. The body, which is a sacred but temporary vehicle, is shed like a snake's skin when it is time for our soul to move on to our next experience of *living*. The love and experience we gain throughout our lifetimes stay with us forever.

Ultimately, uncertainty is our friend. Being in control, knowing all the answers, and having it all planned out is what the ego strives for, but eventually we all learn that this is not where our safety resides. Living in the moment, embracing the unknown, and having faith in the guidance of our Higher Selves are where our true security and power lie. This is the only way to achieve the quality of detachment that allows us to continue our spiritual ascent.

Several years ago, my husband and I went trekking in the Himalayas. We happened to be passing through a remote monastery on the day that the lama was receiving an audience. We had the opportunity to ask him what advice he would have us take back to the United States. Through a translator, he told us: "The difficulty with the West is that most people are too attached. They don't understand that everything is temporary, ephemeral. When times are good, they are happy. When times are hard, they become angry or depressed. When you accept that constant change is the way of life, then you do not attach yourself to everything. This is where peace is found."

I thought about that for a few days, and I remembered that the monks of the monastery seemed "flat" by my own emotional standards. They appeared peaceful and content enough, but were they happy? Was the lama saying that feeling joy was just setting us up for feeling sorrow? And was that to be avoided? Were the ups and downs of our undisciplined minds preventing us from making spiritual progress, or was this the path of *contrast* that we came here to experience fully?

After years of contemplating this, I came to the conclusion that there are multiple good ways to approach life. If your path is to achieve the quiet joy that comes with peace of mind and ultimate detachment from the ups and downs of life, then Buddhism or a similar spiritual practice may be right for you. On the other hand, if your path is one of reveling in the full range of colors, flavors, textures, emotions, and experiences of life, then you may not choose to strive for the same level of detachment.

Life doesn't have to be an all or nothing proposition. You can live a full, rich, passionate existence without the roller coaster ride that often accompanies it. You can accept that everything changes, and set your intentions without being attached to a particular outcome. Faith is the bottom line. When you have faith in your Higher Self and the divine, you no longer need to grasp at anything, and you gain your freedom. It doesn't mean that you won't occasionally question or lose your faith, especially in the face of a seemingly devastating event, but you will recover more quickly, because you have a foundation that you had previously forgotten was there.

The experience of parenthood is one of the greatest teachers of detachment. After the birth of my twins, I experienced extreme anxiety and fear that something tragic would happen to them. Since they were perfectly healthy, safe, and well provided for, all I could think of to do was pray and surrender my fears to God. I did this night after night, and after several weeks of this, I began to change. I became stronger, and my faith grew exponentially because my ego was loosening its grip on my babies, and my Higher Self was stepping forward.

The Higher Self loves without the sticky attachment of the ego. The Higher Self knows that babies have their own angels to watch over them and that parents are stewards and caregivers, but do not control the destiny of their children. Eventually I came to accept the physical world reality that even if something did happen to my children, we would all ultimately be fine. Nothing in this world can separate souls who are bound by love, and if we want to truly love our children, or anyone, without the stifling grip of fear, we must release our ego's attachment to them and allow them the space to have their own experiences.

Applying the Laws of Intention and Detachment

Putting these laws to work in your life requires first that you be present in the *now* moment, which is where your true power lies. Having an intention and releasing it to the universe means trusting that the universe knows more about manifesting your good than your ego does. When you have a strong, sustained, heartfelt intention, and when you are not attached to the outcome, your personal quantum field shifts, influencing the larger quantum field, which may then deliver the fruits of your intention. You don't have to understand the mechanics of this process to recognize the truth in it.

The intention process is simple, but not always easy. It depends on what you believe is *possible*. For instance, you might believe that you can easily manifest a nice vacation, new clothes, or good friends, and therefore, you regularly do. If you believed that there was never enough money or that people were not to be trusted, then these wishes would be difficult for you to manifest. This goes for anything you believe or don't believe to be possible.

Bill Gates and Warren Buffet are examples of financially successful people who were not just in the right place at the right time. They created or *allowed* their wealth and power to flow to them by applying the spiritual laws, whether they were consciously aware of them or not. For them, manifesting a yacht is probably no more difficult than manifesting a toaster. That intention-based power may or may not translate to other areas of their lives, such as relationships, health, and emotional well-being, but in the area of financial success, as

Abraham-Hicks would say, they are "tapped in, tuned in and turned on."[3] Paddling upstream they are not.

Applying the law of detachment requires that we relinquish much of our ego's control over the people and situations in our lives. It requires that we learn to allow others to be who they are, even if it feels threatening or uncomfortable. We can learn to have faith in the orchestrating intelligence of the universe, to embrace uncertainty, and to anticipate miraculous solutions and outcomes that we never could have predicted.

You needn't tackle this all at once. Maybe begin with something small, like refraining from commenting on your teenager's outfit, or perhaps challenging your habitual response to the unknown. When you feel the impulse to "take charge," try stepping back and letting someone else have a turn. Be prepared for your ego to point out how you could have done it better, but you might just be surprised to discover how smoothly things go when you maintain an attitude of detached involvement. You still care about what happens, but you see the wisdom and experience the benefits of going with flow.

THIRTEEN

The Law of Dharma

*D*harma is a Sanskrit word meaning "purpose in life."
According to the law of dharma, you, as a purely
spiritual being, have taken a particular physical body,
at a particular place and time, to fulfill a particular function or
functions. Whether we recognize them or not, we each possess unique talents and predispositions with which to fulfill
our life purposes and thereby serve the universe.

The law of dharma can be broken down into three components, the first of which is discovering one's *true self*, which
goes by many names: Higher Self, God-Self, soul, spirit, etc.
The second component is to identify and express our unique
gifts. We all have God-given talents, each and every one of
us, and it is our job to express these in the world. The third
component is *service*.

Eckhart Tolle offers the following explanation: "Your
life has an inner purpose and an outer purpose. Inner purpose concerns Being and is primary. Outer purpose concerns

doing and is secondary...Inner and outer, however, are so intertwined that it is almost impossible to speak of one without referring to the other."[1] Your inner purpose and my inner purpose are the same, and that is to *awaken* spiritually. To awaken and remember who we are is the collective purpose of humanity, as well as the purpose of this book.

While what we *do* is important for many reasons, who we *are* and who we believe we are is ultimately of greater importance. For instance, with the right state of mind, your grandfather could be occupying a bed in a convalescent hospital while simultaneously generating more good for humanity than a thousand well-intended war protesters who are operating out of fear and anger.

Your inner purpose remains the same throughout your life, while your outer purpose can change over time. This is important to recognize, as many people believe that their outer purpose should permeate their entire life and should feel important. Some people, like Michelangelo, Mozart, and Einstein, come in with such a strongly felt, ironclad outer purpose that it consumes them throughout their entire lives. While others drift through life, never sure of what they came here to do, never feeling that sense of deep inner meaning.

Like it or not, many of us have subtle, but nonetheless crucial, purposes. Consider your favorite grocery store clerk or bank teller whose beautiful warmth and good humor always brighten your day. Her customers are her *ministry*, and her purpose is important to the whole, even if she feels she is contributing little. God needs good people in *every* field, so don't feel that you have to perform an extraordinary task to be in service of humanity. When you do what you love and you do it *with* love, you're right where the universe needs you the most.

Often times discovering and living your inner purpose lays the groundwork for fulfilling your outer purpose, and identifying and honoring that purpose, whatever it is, may be the basis for true success and happiness. We often miss our obvious calling because it doesn't seem important enough or challenging enough. What comes naturally to you may seem too easy, may feel like a cop-out, especially if you've been fed a steady diet of "hard work" mentality.

Perhaps your father struggled and his father struggled just to make ends meet, and as a result of that programming, it's inconceivable to you that your passion for baking could lead to a successful and soul-nourishing career of service to humanity. Perhaps instead you enroll in business school and end up in a job that, while perfectly suited for someone else, is soul deadening for you. What went wrong? You thought you were making a sensible decision, but "sensible" doesn't fulfill your divine life purpose.

Maybe, just maybe, your life purpose is about joyfully and lovingly *feeding* the bodies and souls who travel across town so that they can bring your heavenly bread into their homes and share it with the people they love. Humanity needs good people in every field, and every job is a potential ministry.

The primary problem I see with identifying our outer purpose lies in our childhood conditioning. Virtually every child you know openly displays his natural talents and passions. Some are very physical; some are extremely creative; some are naturally caring and compassionate; some are musically inclined; some love animals; some are intellectual, while others love to make friends and influence people.

Take a moment to think about yourself as a child. Who were you? What did you love to do? What were you naturally good at doing? Is what you're doing now an extension of those early inclinations, and do you love what you do? If you were like most children, you let the opinions and attitudes of the people around you influence your direction. How could you not?

The other night I met with a husband and wife who were in the process of launching their eighteen-year-old twin boys. Both parents were highly successful professionals, and they were concerned that their sons find successful and productive careers. One of the boys was clear about what college he wanted to attend and what field of study he wanted to pursue, but the other boy was lost and confused. He thought maybe he'd look into chemical engineering (his father's profession).

With the law of dharma in mind, I felt compelled to ask the couple what their son loved to do. They both became animated with stories of how he loved to spend time in the garden. They could hardly get him to come indoors (except to play video games, which was his way of zoning out). When he was younger, they bought him a small tractor, with which he spent all of his free time pushing dirt around in the backyard. The couple laughed as they recalled how much he loved being covered with dirt.

I suggested that perhaps their son's natural inclination was to somehow work with the earth. The mother smirked and said, "So you think *our* son should be a *farmer!*" Clearly this thought was unacceptable to her. I went on to explain that while there's certainly nothing wrong with being a farmer, there are countless other career choices that involve being in contact with nature, and that I would be concerned if their son chose a career path that required him to sit in an airtight office building all day long. The mother went on to say that she didn't believe in all this "*passion* business," and that as long as her son found a respectable profession that he "didn't hate" that would do just fine.

My guess is that this boy's lack of direction, as well as escapism through video games, is largely the result of his natural inclinations being rejected within his family. Of course, they love him and want the best for him, but getting one's hands dirty is not their idea of a career track, and no doubt he realizes that all too well.

Try as I might, I was never able to move the mom past her firmly held work ethic that disregards what you love in favor of what you should do or what seems the most "appropriate." Of course, the law of dharma says that what you love *is* what you should do, and it *is* the appropriate choice, no matter how it looks to others. What's more, the universe tends to rush money and support to those who are happily living their purpose without internal conflict. When you're aligned with the laws of the universe, there's no way to stop your God-given abundance from finding you.

Some would disagree. Often you hear people say that they can't make money doing their art, their music, their healing practice. They have to work a day job just to pay the rent. But do you hear the poverty consciousness in that? It's not the art that fails to bring abundance—it's the limited thinking about the art. After all, the starving artist archetype is firmly etched in our minds. Virtually everyone *agrees* that it's impossible to make a decent living as an artist or musician. Didn't your parents prepare you for this harsh "reality"? If not, certainly you've encountered this consciousness repeatedly along the way.

People who go to law school, medical school, or get an MBA are expected to succeed. Whether they do it for love or for money, we *expect* them to succeed. What's special about these financially successful people is not that they are intelligent or hardworking, even though they often are, but that they are in alignment with their success, with their natural abundance. They may or may not end up loving what they do—that's another story—but at their core, perhaps without even knowing it, they were programmed for this kind of success. Otherwise, they would have dropped out or sabotaged themselves along the way.

You never hear a medical student say, "Well, if I can't make it as a dermatologist, I can always sell skin care products, or I can move back in with my parents." People who intend to succeed in a given field generally don't have a back-up plan. They may not succeed at every turn, but they don't *plan* for failure. The same holds true for the artist, the actor, the musician, or the energy worker who *succeeds*. They expect to do so, and they don't let society tell them otherwise.

Another not-so-obvious piece is that sometimes we don't make money directly from our "art," but the universe sends abundance to support us through other channels. For instance, a friend of mine has always followed her passion, whether it be attending design school, training to be an energy worker, having children, starting a baking company, or writing. For better or worse, it never occurred to her to ask the question, "How can I make money?," and making money was never her strong suit. For a long time, she was disappointed in herself because of this until she realized that the universe had been supporting her abundantly all along.

One way or another, she had always attracted everything she needed: love, money, support, friendship. The only thing she ever lacked was self-esteem. The way she saw herself made her feel unsuccessful, but once she began to awaken to her true spiritual essence, she realized that through her sincere commitment to being of service and following her heart she had been supported by the universe. Inadvertently, my friend had manifested great abundance through the law of dharma.

Working with the Law of Dharma

How do you apply the law of dharma? First, focus on who you are inside, your true nature as a spiritual being, because no matter what your outer purpose is, it is best served by a conscious person who is aware of his place in the grander scheme of the universe. So go for long walks in nature, meditate, journal, or repeatedly ask yourself the question, "Who am I?" But most importantly, allow yourself the space to just *be*, without any pressure to make progress on your spiritual path, because your true nature is only revealed in the present moment.

Next, ask yourself the following questions: What do I love to do? If money and time were of no concern to me, how would I spend my days? What are my natural gifts? What do people tell me about myself? Be sure to include and validate feedback such as: "You're a great listener," "You're a wonderful dad," and "You're always so positive and encouraging."

Once you've become clear about what you'd like to do, begin to consider how you can utilize your gifts to serve humanity, the earth, or the universe. Remember that "service" is an extremely broad category. Your purpose can include being a financially successful salesperson who is always looking out for the highest good of her customers. You can provide a divine service by treating them well and staying in your integrity. The world needs good-hearted salespeople as much as it needs loving nurses or soup kitchen volunteers. And there's nothing wrong with wanting to manifest abundance.

Finally, remember that you have a team of spirit helpers whose job it is to guide you, when asked, and that they can see the larger picture of how your life purpose plugs into the greater purposes of the universe. They *want* you to succeed, not only for your own good, but for the good of all that is. You are a critical piece of the grand puzzle, so when you have an attack of feeling like you're too small to do that great thing you've been dreaming of doing, remember that you would not be guided to do it if the higher powers, including your own Higher Self, didn't believe that you were capable of it. If you can't push past your perceived limitations for yourself, do it for your loved ones, do it for humanity, do it for God.

PART III

Going The Distance

GOING THE DISTANCE

In the previous discussion of dharma, we took a good look at the importance of tuning into one's natural inclinations as they relate to finding and following one's divine life purpose. In the next chapter, we will continue to explore the topic of knowing oneself, and then move on to some powerful energy work practices. These techniques will help you release what no longer serves you, and further activate your spiritual path.

Please read through to the end of the book, and return later to the exercises that best fit for you. This way you'll have a broader perspective of where you're going and what areas you may need to focus on to get there.

FOURTEEN

Knowing Who You Are

Know thyself. Why is this so important, and why is it so difficult? How is it possible to go through life, to live with ourselves day in and day out, and not be clear about who we are? As human beings, sometimes the key to discovering who we are lies in realizing who we are *not,* and living in a world of contrasts helps us do just that.

There are a myriad of ways in which human life can lead us astray, and we came here knowing that we would lose our way and have to find it again. We came here to experience, firsthand, the illusion of separation from source, which is the root of all of our problems, illnesses, pain, and suffering.

If you are reading books like this, you will have already traveled quite a distance on the road of self-discovery, but in this chapter you will be asked to take it a few steps further. Whatever illusion you still hold about who you are, and who others are, is standing between you and your spiritual destiny. Whatever false self you may have adopted as a small child will need to be exposed. This does not mean that it must be dis-mantled or destroyed, but simply exposed for what it is. The truth will set you free.

Before we move on to some exercises and practices for knowing ourselves better, let's look at a few common ways in which people have learned to relate to themselves and their world. These are coping mechanisms for living with the amnesia of having forgotten who we really are.

As human beings, we are born with limitations. We are wholly dependent on our parents or others for our survival, and as infants, we quickly tune into these people's fears, inse-curities, and other unhealed issues. If our parents are basically healthy, well-adjusted, and welcoming of us, we will probably get what we need in order to move forward in our lives in a *normal* fashion. We'll still have our struggles, but the founda-tion will be in place.

If, on the other hand, we are raised by a parent (or two) who has a significant mental or emotional issue, compulsion, addiction, personality disorder, illness, disability, etc., then most likely we will be impacted in some important way. While it might seem unfair that some children are born into happy homes, while others suffer miserable circumstances, by now we are recognizing that we purposely chose our parents and siblings, as well as cultural and socioeconomic circumstances, in order to facilitate our growth in certain areas.

For instance, if we chose to be born into an alcoholic or abusive home, it was for the purpose of learning lessons that those environments could best teach. It's easy to blame our parents for our shortcomings, but ultimately we must take responsibility for our own choices.

Understanding the Lower Self

As souls, we come into bodies and form relationships with ourselves that will last a lifetime. This relationship can change over time, but is based on our early assessment of who we are. As young children, if things go well and we are comfortable enough in our own skin, we will move forward in our development in an unobstructed manner. We will develop a healthy, realistic self-image that takes into account our human strengths and weaknesses. We may not love everything about ourselves, but we possess a healthy acceptance of who we are.

If, for whatever reason, we are not comfortable with who we think we are, we may attempt to re-create ourselves internally. This can take on any number of forms, but let's look at a couple of the most common manifestations.

When a child has forgotten his true spiritual identity and doesn't like whom he sees in the mirror, he may create an *idealized self*. This is a "digitally enhanced" image of himself that is perhaps smarter, better looking, more confident, and more successful than his ordinary, flawed self. While not even this idealized self holds a candle to the greatness of who he really is, this is the lower self's attempt to compensate for his perceived inadequacy.

Sadly, the idealized self construct is a setup for failure, at least in the short-term, because it can lead us either into a personality pattern of neurosis or narcissism, both of which can range from mild to severe. While these psychological terms can feel worn-out and pathologizing (the movie *Annie Hall* comes to mind), they do a good job of helping us understand some important psychological concepts.

Neurosis

A *neurotic* personality is someone whose sense of self is basically intact, but is wounded and deficient. He experiences shame and guilt, for many reasons, but perhaps mainly for having forgotten who he is and inadvertently having turned his back on God. He struggles to feel empowered and worthy. He worries about what others think of him and is very self-critical. While not selfish, per se, he is quite self-absorbed. If something goes wrong, it must be his fault. His wounding may range from a nagging sense of not being up to snuff to being chronically depressed and self-loathing.

From this deficient self is born an idealized self-image that gives the neurotic personality hope. If he works hard to be "better," he believes he will eventually overcome his deficiencies and become worthy. The problem is that this manufactured, idealized version of himself is not who he really is at all. It is not real and is thus unattainable. No matter how hard he tries, he will never become the person he pictures in his mind, and the very pursuit of this idealized self cuts him off from remembering who he really is and experiencing his true, which is to say spiritual, potential.

As long as he rejects the fallible human being that he is, he cannot step into the reality of his Higher Self. Just as there is inherent beauty and courage in the awkward child who repeatedly falls as she's learning to walk, so is there beauty and honor in the seemingly ordinary, flawed human being who steadfastly perseveres on his path, in spite of its many challenges. Ironically, when we honor ourselves *with* our limitations, we make it possible to move past them.

Narcissism

A *narcissistic* personality is someone whose basic sense of self has not been nurtured, and in effect, this self is hanging by a thread. The stereotypical culprit is a cold, distant mother who is unable or unwilling to nurture her baby, leaving her alone in her crib to cry it out. Because the real self is shriveled and undeveloped, the child conjures up a powerful idealized self that she believes to be who she really is.

While the neurotic personality is constantly comparing the ideal self to the deficient "real" self and coming up short, the narcissistic personality has bought into the image of the idealized self lock, stock, and barrel. She has manufactured an inflated, godlike, false self that she believes to be who she really is. In her mind, she is smarter, more talented, and of higher quality than other lesser mortals, even despite evidence to the contrary.

Not unlike the neurotic person, the narcissist sees herself as the center of the universe and is self-absorbed. In each case, we can clearly see the ego at work. Unlike the neurotic person, the narcissist sees herself as bigger than life. She doesn't have the problem; everybody else does. She has an oversized sense of self-importance and entitlement and is perplexed when others resist getting with her program.

A "successful" narcissist can keep the illusion of self going for years, while a less effective personality will experience the false self inflating and deflating like a balloon, which can be disruptive. She will not understand the reason for the failures and will blame others for the divorce, the job loss, the bankruptcy. With great effort and motivation, it is possible for the shriveled sense of authentic self to grow, but this requires that huge internal shifts occur.

Psychosis

So far we have discussed three broad categories: healthy relationship with self and world, neurotic relationship with self and world, and narcissistic relationship with self and world. Beyond this we find a host of increasingly unhealthy configurations of self, ranging from borderline to full-blown psychotic personalities. While neurotic and narcissistic personality types represent some injury to self and neglect to self, psychotic personalities represent a devastating injury to the self. The Higher Self may remain intact, but the lower human-level self is all but shattered.

The reason for outlining the human *psychological* situation is that we are humans who are prone to falling into certain psychological traps. When we see the trap for what it is, we can begin to set ourselves free of it.

For instance, if you're a consistently straight A student who feels that failure is always just around the next corner, you may be suffering from an unrealistic expectation of perfection that is based on an idealized self-image. While having high standards is great, this is ultimately a setup for failure, because human beings are not perfect. As long as we chase human perfection (in ourselves or others) we are missing the point of the human situation, which is to evolve through experience, and we are distracting ourselves from accessing our true greatness, which is spiritually based.

So the first exercise in knowing oneself is to determine where you fit in the above scheme. Do you experience a mostly healthy relationship to self? Have you worked through a neurotic pattern or a narcissistic pattern of relationship to self and world? Do you see of a little of each? Be honest with yourself. Look at where you've been and where you are now. If you still see yourself as better or worse than others, take some time to explore the roots of these perceptions. You might still be operating from a self-image you set up during early childhood, which may have served you well at the time, but is now obsolete. Be willing to observe yourself honestly, and surrender to God whatever you no longer need. You don't have to fix yourself. Just be willing to release what no longer benefits you, so you can move on.

What Does Your Personality Tell You?

As we've already discussed, our personalities can be the portal to our souls. The human persona is the tip of the iceberg of our greater spiritual personality and can help us remember who we are and what we came here to accomplish. For instance, if you are naturally extroverted and love to network and meet new people, you can be sure that these qualities reflect your soul's purpose and function. You may be a bridger, an up-lifter, a way shower, a speaker, a promoter, a politician, etc. You may want a partner who loves to go on adventures with you, or you may be attracted to your opposite.

On the other hand, if you are introverted, love to journal, connect deeply with close friends and family members, and go on long, contemplative walks in nature, your purpose and divine function will be different. You may also be a way shower and up-lifter, but you will approach it in a different way than the extrovert would, which is appropriate. You may find that inspirational writing, one-on-one counseling or energy work, or studying nature suits you well. You may want a mellow partner who respects your "space" or possibly someone more energetic who draws you out.

If you are interested in understanding yourself and others more deeply, there are several good personality-typing systems out there that can help you uncover who you are at the personality level and beyond. My favorite system is the *Enneagram* because it is ancient and spiritually based, but most of all because it is ingenious and has helped me understand myself and others in a way that no other system has.

Some might say, "I'm unique—I won't be pigeon-holed or put in a box," but the truth is that if we're human beings with personalities, we're already in a box; we just don't realize it. We think that our perception of the world is "reality." We vaguely believe that everyone perceives, or *should* perceive life the same way we do, and we are mystified by the strange things that others say and do.

Only when we realize that we have been operating with blinders on can we step back, remove the blinders, and see things from a broader perspective. This is tremendously freeing, and when we start to recognize the particular brand of blinders *others* are wearing, we can begin to understand them better, and our relationships with friends, family, and people we don't know improve greatly.

It is believed that the Enneagram originated in the Sufi teachings, although others claim that it cropped up independently in other parts of the world. Until recently, it was strictly an oral tradition, taught only through interaction with people, but now we can learn its principles by way of the written word.

The Enneagram is depicted by a nine-pointed star diagram, each point representing a personality type. While we each possess all nine qualities to some degree, there is one that we are more *fixated* on than the others. Generally, this focus or fixation is most easily seen when a person is in his twenties, while he's still searching for himself. The nine personality fixations or types include:

Point 1:   Perfectionist
Point 2:   Helper/Giver
Point 3:   Achiever/Performer
Point 4:   Artist/Romantic
Point 5:   Observer/Intellectual
Point 6:   Loyalist/Devil's Advocate
Point 7:   Epicure/Free Spirit
Point 8:   Boss/Leader
Point 9:   Mediator

By studying all of these types, we start to understand and appreciate the basic personality *templates* that comprise humanity. This is true not only for individuals, but also for families, political groups, companies, countries, etc.

For instance, the United States as a whole expresses the performer/achiever, while Italy expresses the artist/romantic, and Switzerland expresses the perfectionist. This doesn't mean that every citizen of these countries represents that type, but that the overall tenor of that country's culture expresses it.

So the fixation that we have helps us understand what we need to work on, because the goal is to loosen this preoccupation so that it doesn't take over our lives. Ideally the fixation (the drive to achieve, to be loved, to be in charge, etc.) will be transformed or transmuted into its higher spiritual counterpart (to simply "be," to love unconditionally, to be a great leader, etc.).

Being familiar with these personality archetypes is like being familiar with the spiritual laws. They provide a blueprint to help you understand the structure that you're operating within. If you don't relate to something, or disagree with something on the blueprint, you can disregard it or throw it away, but at least you have a starting place. You don't have to start from ground zero. These and many other blueprints (spiritual texts, astrology, numerology, etc.) are given to us as gifts from spirit to provide a foothold on our journey up the mountain.

If you've never studied personality types, you might be amazed at the ways in which this information can help you make sense of your life, past and present. Helen Palmer's book, *The Enneagram: Understanding Yourself and the Others in Your Life*, is a classic, which I heartily recommend, but there are other simpler books to choose from as well. In fact, there are many personality systems and resources available, so let your guidance steer you toward the material that works best for you.

Discovering Your Preferences

The discussion of what we like and what we dislike might seem rudimentary for where you are at this stage. Even a toddler knows that she loves her blanky, but can't stand lima beans. As adults, we know that we love our children, but loathe paying income tax. Besides, aren't we trying to be accepting and nonjudgmental?

While this is true, it is also true that many of us have become desensitized and confused about our needs and preferences. The toddler may be crystal clear about wanting a little red car, but what about the adult?

The adult thought process might go something like this: "I really want a red sports car. Red. That would be great…or maybe I'd get a black one. I hear red cars get more speeding tickets. I don't want to be worrying about that all the time. What I *should* get is a four seater. They're more practical and less expensive. Maybe I'll get a sedan in red—I mean black. That would make the most sense. I could do that. In fact, that's what I really want. I don't need a sports car at all. Ooh, look at that red Corvette…!"

Several years ago when my twins were two or three years old, I occasionally had the opportunity to go out alone, for fun, and do whatever I wanted to do. I had been so accustomed to taking care of everyone else that I had no idea what I wanted to do with my free time. It was as if part of my brain had been removed and I couldn't remember what I used to do to amuse myself. I'd ask myself, "What do I want to do?" and there was just blankness and eerie silence.

I asked my Higher Self to help me get back in touch with myself, and something fascinating happened. I started hearing a little, seemingly primitive, inner voice that would occasionally say, "I love that," or "I hate that." You might not think this sounds sophisticated or desirable, but I was thrilled.

153

That little, childlike voice was crystal clear about what it liked and didn't like, what it wanted to do and what it didn't want to do. It was only then that I realized I had gone through most of my life without realizing what I wanted. I knew the basics, the big things, but I had never bothered to ask myself about the details.

One day I said to my husband, "I've been starting to think about my likes and dislikes. For instance, I have no idea what my dream home would look like." He looked at me, a little surprised, and said, "Honey, your dream home is like a Victorian Bed and Breakfast with a big, flowery garden." He was right. That was my dream home, and I hadn't even realized it. It was humbling to me that my husband knew more about what I liked than I did.

As an exercise, make a list of your likes and dislikes. Perhaps write about this in your journal. Or as you go through the day, check in with yourself about how you feel regarding the people, places, and things you come in contact with. The point is not to throw around judgments but to discern your authentic thoughts and feelings about these aspects of life. Once you are clear about your preferences, it becomes easier to move beyond them and learn to accept life just the way it is.

Journaling

Another important aspect of knowing oneself is being able to identify our feelings. If you've ever cried (or exploded) over "spilled milk," you know what happens when we don't manage our feelings and stress. Someone who is practiced in the art of identifying and releasing emotions is rarely caught off guard by her own unexpected and exaggerated *reactions*. We will talk more about *clearing* built-up emotions in the next chapter, but with regard to identifying and getting familiar with our emotional landscape, there's perhaps no better way to do this than journaling.

As we've discussed, not everyone is a good candidate for journaling—for one reason or another—but if you do find it beneficial to write out your thoughts and feelings, you will be amazed at the wisdom and clarity you gain from this most valuable tool.

Whenever I find myself feeling confused, depressed, irritable, or tense, I know it is time to sit down with my journal and just *write*. It usually starts out with, "I don't know why I'm feeling so…" Usually within twenty minutes I'm not only clear about what's been bothering me, but I've received guidance from my Higher Self about what to do, and the acute distress is 90–100 percent resolved. It's like magic.

At the beginning of each journaling session, it is a good idea to apply some sort of psychic protection, like visualizing yourself surrounded with light, saying a prayer, or calling in your angels. The reason for this is that journaling, like meditating, can open us up, and we don't want to be left vulnerable to outside influences.

While there are countless journaling styles and techniques, one of the most powerful tricks I've found is to be willing to start out *foolish* and finish *wise*. What does that mean? When you start out foolish, you're saying, "I admit that I don't know what the heck is going on. I'm behaving badly, being a drama queen. I thought I had made a lot of progress, but apparently I have not. God, please help me sort this out!" By honestly expressing how you really feel in the present moment and surrendering it to God, you are opening the door to the channeling of your highest guidance. This is what is meant by being willing to "finish wise."

The problem that some people face with journaling is that they approach it in a lopsided fashion. Either they are too formal and present their thoughts as if they already have it all together, as if the lower self does not require a voice or even exist, or they spew endlessly from the lower self perspective without ever inviting the Higher Self to weigh in. The real benefit comes from giving each side a voice. At some point, the lower self will become transformed and merged with the Higher Self, but until then, it is important to let it express itself. This is one of the important ways in which the ego becomes healed and integrated.

Inner Voice Dialogue

The lower self is made up of many ego subpersonalities, and the Higher Self may express as different voices. While it is not necessary to identify and name all of these inner voices, it is important to recognize where they are coming from. By journaling with these various voices, you will quickly sort out what's what. The Higher Self and its team of colleagues (divinely sanctioned angels, ascended masters, spirit guides, etc.) will sound and feel loving and wise, while the lower self subpersonalities will have "issues." They might sound all right at first, but will eventually reveal an agenda that is based on fear or self-preservation. The Higher Self has no fear.

In your journal, you can catalog these personalities as they appear. If you give them your attention, they will probably be more than willing to present themselves. For instance, if you detect and angry inner voice, you might ask, "Who are you, and what are you so upset about?" Most likely you will start receiving information, which may be general or may be specific, but if you follow it in, without resisting the message, you will get to the core of it fairly quickly.

Allow each subpersonality to express itself, and dialogue with it, either in your mind or in your journal. Step into, or align with, the Higher Self in order to respond effectively to the needs of the particular subpersonality. If, however, you should feel that a voice does not belong to some aspect of *you*, as is often the case for individuals with addictions or other mental disturbances, ask spirit to remove this "entity" immediately. We do not accommodate, or negotiate with, lower energies that do not belong to us.

Eventually most, if not all, of your inner voices and guides will present themselves. If you sense that one of these sub-personalities is hiding from view, perhaps a shy or frightened inner child, feel free to ask your Higher Self to help you call forth this personality. This exercise may help you understand and fill in the blanks of your emotional life.

An advanced version of this exercise can be found in Elizabeth Gilbert's book, *Eat, Pray, Love*. The author had been experiencing an acute emotional crisis and had just spent several days alone, in silence, when she asked her inner self to reveal itself to her fully. She said, "...Show me everything that is causing you sorrow...anger...shame...show me your worst." One by one each painful feeling, experience, and sub-personality presented itself for healing, and following each one, she would say, "It's okay. I love you. I accept you. Come into my heart now."[1] It took hours and hours, but eventually every voice, every bit of suffering, had been revealed and acknowledged. Finally, her mind was at peace.

Channeling Higher Guidance

As you become more proficient in your journaling practices, you may find that Higher Self starts coming through on its own. Perhaps you are expressing your frustration about some issue, and then you notice that a shift has occurred. Maybe the issue starts to fade from consciousness, and you find yourself writing words of wisdom to yourself. Or you might find that you're ranting effusively about something, and then the energy suddenly vanishes, leaving you sitting there, pen in hand, wondering how to finish the sentence.

With practice, you can sit down, anytime, anywhere, and *channel* your higher guidance, which means getting your lower self out of the way so that higher guidance can flow through you. While it's possible to channel guidance from angels, ascended masters, and other spirit guides, keep in mind that the answers to all your questions already exist within you.

You can enjoy and benefit from interaction with divinely sanctioned higher-level guides, but avoid the temptation to defer to them or see them as your superiors. We are all sparks of the divine. They are there to help us along when we have forgotten that, but once we've plugged into our Higher Self, we have everything we need.

Over the last few decades, many people have begun channeling individual entities or group entities. Some popular examples include Lee Carroll's *Kryon*, Esther Hicks' *Abraham*, and *The Group* channeled by Steve Rother. These particular

beings, and many others, have served a great purpose in edu-
cating and spiritually uplifting millions of people around the
world, and it was their shared purpose to do so, but we should
always exercise discernment when considering information
channeled by ourselves or others.

This is true for several reasons. First of all, not every
being who wants to be channeled is wise and benevolent.
People sometimes believe that just because a spirit is on the
other side, it must have clear vision and thus possess wisdom.
There's a saying, "Just because they're dead, doesn't mean
they're smart." Not all channelable beings are created equal.

Secondly, when human beings channel information, the
information passes through the individual's personal filters.
She may or may not be able to express it faithfully, and her
own thoughts, feelings, personal agenda, and/or physical state
may affect the transmission. The channel is human, after all.

Finally, even if the channeled information is of the highest quality, it may not be true for you. This is why it is critical
to always check in with yourself with regard to any input you
receive, whether it comes from the eleven o'clock news or
your most highly esteemed guru. What is relevant information for others may not be relevant to you.

Ultimately we are moving in the direction of operating
entirely from our Higher Self perspective, which means that
we will no longer search for answers outside of ourselves.
We will not need to channel ascended masters or Higher
Self because we will be operating *from* our Higher Self.
We will *be* it.

Until then, however, it can be of great value to tap into
and channel the highest aspects of your being whenever

possible. The more you do this, the higher your vibration will become, and the more you will remember who you really are.

Honoring the Person You Are

There are thousands of practices, exercises, therapies, articles, books, and Web sites out there that are designed to help you understand and know yourself better. There are even more resources available to help you "improve" yourself, which you may have been working on extensively for years. For this week or this month, please consider dropping all efforts to be a *better* person and focus your attention on learning more about, and honoring, the person you are right here and right now.

Ask yourself, "Who am I?" and see what thoughts come to you. You might hear yourself answer, "I'm a plumber," "I'm a housewife," "I'm a Catholic," or "I'm a singer." Take a moment to go a little deeper. Are some of these just the roles that you play, and others profound aspects of who you are inside? Perhaps being a housewife is a temporary role, whereas being a singer is reflective of your divine life purpose. If you hear answers like, "I'm a child of God," or "I'm a spark of the divine," then you'll know that you're no longer operating from the perspective of the roles you play.

Take time to honor the human being that you are, with all your warts and bruises, with all your unpaid bills and "failed" relationships. The fact that you're here in the first place means that you're a pretty remarkable being. Take a moment to push aside any criticism you have of yourself, any regrets from the past or doubts about the future. Like Stuart Smalley from *Saturday Night Live* used to do: take a deep breath, smile, and say, "I'm good enough, I'm smart enough, and doggonit, people like me!" If we can keep our senses of humor, it's not too hard to laugh at the bumbling mistakes we humans make. Trying to be perfect or to be someone that we're not can ruin all of our fun.

FIFTEEN

Working with Energy

We are human beings living in a material world, but beyond this, we are *energetic* beings. What animates and defines us, what makes us who we are, is the spirit composition that is our soul. While we may often be fooled by appearances, the material world and our physical bodies are nothing more than direct expressions of energy.

Any ailment you have is the manifestation of some difficulty, blockage, or imbalance on an energetic level. Any pollution, poverty, or war is an expression of the same. While our physical bodies are separate and distinct, our energetic bodies know no definite bounds and can be projected outward indefinitely. What this means is that every person, every entity, every conflict, everywhere is connected to you in some way and has the potential to affect you. This is especially true for what's going on within about a half-mile radius of you and regarding people with whom you are emotionally connected, but you are also affected by a myriad of forces outside of your awareness.

In addition to these external influences, you are constantly affected by internal energetic forces and habits of which you may not even be aware. Your perceptions and personal beliefs largely dictate how you perceive yourself, others, and every situation you encounter or create. These personal patterns determine whether you go with the flow or fight everything tooth and nail. These habits take on a life of their own and can be productive or quite destructive.

So we *are* energy, and we run on energy. We each have a sort of energy bank account. Some of us have learned to be good managers of our accounts, while others inadvertently squander their energy and never seem to have enough. They then seek out other people's energy just so they can scrape by. Or perhaps they are *empaths,* people who naturally merge with other people's energy and can become depleted by the resulting roller coaster ride.

You've probably had the experience of feeling drained after a conversation with someone who then reports how much better *she* feels. We unconsciously give energy to, and take energy from, one another all the time, but life becomes so much easier when you have energy *reserves* and are able to give of yourself by your own consent, and in a way that does not sap the living daylights out of you.

We are all energy workers, whether we realize it or not. Whenever you take a deep breath, stop to enjoy a moment, or hug a loved one, you are intuitively replenishing your energy supply in a healthy way. Likewise, when you find yourself sighing deeply, having a good cry, or taking a brisk walk to unwind, you are attempting to clear away unwanted energy or stress, also in a healthy way.

While some of our energy-balancing attempts work well, others are misguided and ultimately fail us. For instance, using food, drugs, alcohol, sex, or any obsessive or compulsive behavior to relieve stress works only briefly and superficially and can lead to much greater problems. Additionally, since like attracts like, addictive energy attracts other addictive energy, including people, situations, and even low-level entities who attach themselves to us for the purpose of feeding on our "highs." These are psychic hitchhikers who encourage us to "use" more and more and can erode our self-esteem and sabotage our work and relationships.

As you can see, protecting your energy and keeping it at the highest vibration possible is important not only to your spiritual growth, but to your very survival. Even the healthiest of us can fall into poor habits and be prone to energy drains. The good news is that by learning and applying some basic energy *clearing, shielding,* and *balancing* techniques, you can safeguard yourself from the energetic ups and downs that so many people experience as "normal" life.

Balancing refers to bringing our energies into harmony such that one part is not neglected while another is overemphasized. *Clearing* means the releasing of accumulated energy that we don't want or need, and *shielding* means protecting and shoring ourselves up so that we are not vulnerable to unwanted influences in the first place. Also critically important is *grounding,* which has different meanings, but for our purposes we will call it being fully present and anchored in one's body, such that we are available to experience what we came here to experience.

165

In the next chapter, we will go further into specific grounding, shielding, and clearing techniques, but first let's discuss the foundations of our energy system: the chakras and the special role of heart. These provide the basis for achieving balance.

The Chakras

Our physical and spiritual aspects unite in the *chakras* or energy centers found in and around the human body. There are seven major energy centers within the body, each residing next to a hormonal gland, as well as seven more that continue upward beyond the top of your head. There are also hundreds of minor chakras, including those in the hands and feet. If you could see chakras, as some people can, they would appear as spinning wheels, cones, or spheres, of colored light.

The function of the chakras is to conduct and circulate life force energy (also known as chi, ki, or prana,) throughout the body, to keep us healthy and charged. However, lower frequency (negative) thoughts and feelings can slow down and darken the chakras, causing mental, emotional, spiritual, and physical problems. For instance, an individual with physical heart problems may be found to have issues related to the heart chakra, which is concerned with giving and/or receiving love. Likewise, someone with chronic or acute throat trouble may be found to have issues with the throat chakra, which regulates communication and self-expression.

The following is a brief description of the major chakras found within the human body. The first three are the lower chakras, starting at the base of the spine, which is the slowest spinning. Chakras four through seven and above are the higher chakras. As the spin increases, the color changes accordingly.

1. *Root Chakra:* Located at the base of the spine. Relates to physical survival, safety, security, money, and career. Ruby red.
2. *Sacral Chakra:* Located halfway between the base of the spine and the navel. An emotional center that relates to creativity, sexuality, health/body issues, appetites, and addictions. Tropical orange.
3. *Solar Plexus Chakra:* Located behind the navel. Relates to all issues of internal and external power and control. Bright yellow.
4. *Heart Chakra:* Located in the center of the chest. Relates to love, forgiveness or unforgiveness, relationships, and attachments with others. The Higher Self expresses through the heart. Emerald green.
5. *Throat Chakra:* Located in the throat area. Relates to all forms of communication, speaking your truth, asserting your needs, expression of self. Sky blue.
6. *Third Eye* or *Brow Chakra:* Located between the eyebrows. Relates to clairvoyance, pictures of the past and future, spiritual beliefs, and vision. Indigo.
7. *Crown Chakra:* Located just inside the top of the head. Relates to thoughts and experiences of God, spirituality and religion, divine direction, and trust in that guidance. Violet or purple.

Approximately seven to nine inches above the head is the eighth chakra, which acts as a "master control" in the transformational processes of spiritual awakening and ascension.

Improperly functioning chakras may appear murky, spotty, or containing holes. In general, a chakra will shrink and appear dirty if we hold fear about that part of ourselves, and the chakra will become disproportionately large if we are obsessed or preoccupied with it. For instance, the solar plexus chakra may become dark and shrunken if we hold thoughts of being a victim in life, but it may become oversized if we are obsessed with asserting our personal power.

The key is to have healthy and balanced chakras, which means that they are all clean, bright in color, uniform in size (6" or larger in diameter), and spinning rapidly in a clockwise direction. In this way, energy can flow through them and throughout our bodies without interruption or blockage.

If you've ever studied Abraham Maslow's Hierarchy of Needs,[1] you'll remember that we humans start out focusing on physical survival (first chakra) and gradually work our way up to spiritual enlightenment (seventh chakra and above). This can take lifetimes, and it is not uncommon to become stuck along the way. But once the lower three chakras are functional, it becomes possible to move up into the heart and begin receiving direct guidance from the Higher Self. People who have not experienced this yet may believe that it does not exist.

Oftentimes spiritual seekers, who have previously progressed up through the chakras, will become so enamored with the higher chakras that they neglect the lower ones, and experience first, second, and/or third chakra imbalances, such as money problems, body issues, or challenges with personal power. In order to be truly healthy and whole, we must attend to all of our major energy centers.

There are many ways to clear and balance your chakras, and since most people accumulate psychic debris, it's not a bad idea to do a quick process every day. If you have not done this before or would like a guided meditation, there are many chakra-clearing CDs available on the market, including a good one by Doreen Virtue.[2]

It's also possible to clear and balance your chakras by simply visualizing them as you would like them to appear and function. In energy work, intention is key. Visualize it, intend it, and it is so. If you do this every day, even for a moment, over time you will see results.

If you have a disease, wound, or other problem area, give that chakra area a little extra care. As difficult as it might seem, do your best to view that area as healthy and well. Like a centrifuge, spin out illness, guilt, resentment, and habitually limiting ways of seeing yourself. This will do wonders in the healing process.

Tashira Tachi-ren presents a powerful exercise called, "Invocation to the Unified Chakra."[3] Generally speaking, in this meditation, one breathes in divine light through the center of the heart, which opens the heart and allows more divine light to enter. With each successive breath the light expands in all directions, gradually enfolding the entire body, from below the feet, up to the fourteenth chakra, in divine light.

When you are done, make sure to ground yourself fully (which will be discussed in the next chapter) before you move forward in your day. This exercise can raise your vibration substantially, as well as shield you from the interference of untoward energies, both internal and external.

Following Your Heart

The heart is perhaps the greatest tool we have for clearing, shielding, and balancing our energy and our physical bodies. In this section, we will discuss how this works, but first let's talk about the *function* of the heart.

In the previous meditation, you were asked to breathe light in through the center of the heart, but what does this mean, given that the word "heart" has so many definitions? Basically, the heart is a bodily organ as well as an intuitive feeling center. It is a major chakra as well as the metaphorical seat of love and goodness.

The heart is the rhythm-setting apparatus for the other organs and for the entire body and mind. The state of the heart, both physical and energetic, sets the tone for how we feel emotionally and how we handle stress, which in turn has a profound effect on our physical and mental health. The heart, whether as a physical organ or as a chief energy center, is a powerful muscle, a significant source of strength and intelligence for humans and animals alike.

On the most basic level, the intuitive intelligence of the heart alerts us to mortal danger, thus triggering the body's fight or flight response system. The heart signals the brain to "think fast" and take immediate action. On a more subtle level, the intelligence of the heart can guide us in every decision we make.

Researchers at the Institute of HeartMath[4] in California discovered the relationship between one's emotional state and the heart rhythm patterns observed when a person is hooked up to an electrocardiogram machine. If you are relaxed, if you feel content, secure, and happy, your heart rhythm is smooth and radiates this pattern to the brain and the rest of the organs, thus setting the tone for the entire system. They call this heart state "coherence," which is another way of saying that you are in alignment with your Higher Self, which expresses through the heart.

Conversely, when you feel tense, distressed, irritated, etc., your heart rhythm is irregular or jagged, like an earthquake presents on a Richter scale, and radiates this signal to the brain and other organs. They call this "incoherence," or what we might call being out of alignment with your Higher Self. If this incoherence is experienced repeatedly over time, it becomes a habitual pattern or *groove* in the brain, and as a result, brain functioning can become altered or impaired. The stress response becomes a sort of default setting, such that the slightest stressor can cause an exaggerated fight-or-flight-like response.

Based on this model, it is easy to see how we can get into a habit of accumulating stress and other emotional and psychic baggage, which in turn lowers our vibration and our resistance to illness and undesirable outside influences. This creates a snowball effect that can take us down if we don't apply some form of energy clearing and balancing practices.

To further demonstrate the powerful influence of the heart, consider this: surrounding each of us is a measurable electromagnetic field made up of the collective fields of the brain, the heart, and all the other electrical systems throughout the body. HeartMath authors Doc Childre and Deborah Rozman, Ph.D., describe the awesome power and intelligence of the heart. They write, "The heart's electromagnetic field has forty to sixty times more amplitude than that of the brain, while the heart's magnetic field is approximately five thousand times stronger than the field produced by the brain. (McCraty 2004)."[5]

When you are in alignment with your heart, you have tremendous strength and power, while being in alignment with your brain alone packs very little punch. When making an important decision, it can be illuminating or therapeutic to make a list of pros and cons, but in the end, what does your heart say? The intelligence of the heart takes all factors, seen and unseen, known and unknown, into account.

So how do we go about employing the heart to clear stress and other unwanted thoughts and emotions, build reserves of nurturing life force energy, repair energy leaks and drains, and reprogram the brain?

As it turns out, this is easier than you might think. Just by focusing your attention on the heart area and taking a few deep breaths, you can quickly redirect attention from the brain or other energy centers to the heart center. I like to put my hand on my heart, as this speeds up the connection and charges it even more, but the mere intention to access the heart puts you in it. There may or may not be a fight from the ego around this, depending on how entrenched you are at any given moment, but the more you practice the easier it gets.

Once you learn to redirect attention to your heart, there are many additional techniques you can use to clear, shield, and balance your energy. Note that most of the following suggestions are based on HeartMath techniques found in the Childre and Rozman book,[6] which I highly recommend.

1. Breathe slowly in through the heart and out through the heart. Or try breathing in through the heart and releasing out through the solar plexus, which is about four inches below the heart.

2. While breathing through the heart, recall a positive experience or feeling, and just be with it. Or focus on feeling genuine gratitude or appreciation. Continue this as long as possible, and quickly come back to the heart if your attention wanders. This can last half a minute, five minutes, fifteen minutes, or longer. This exercise can be used as a quick fix when you're upset, as a technique for building reserves of calming energy, and as a technique for setting a new and more functional groove in the brain.

3. While breathing through the heart, ask your heart to show you what would make you feel better or what you need to know in this moment. Sometimes you can't conjure up a good feeling of your own, but your heart is always ready to go. (The first time I tried this I received an instant "slide show" of scenes that were both emotionally soothing and brought everything I was experiencing into to perspective. It was like magic.)

4. While breathing through the heart, focus on an attitude or state of mind that you'd like to foster. For example, if you are upset with yourself or someone else, you might breathe in forgiveness. You can then breathe out forgiveness through the solar plexus, or if

necessary, blow out the upset through the mouth. This can quickly release negative feelings from your body. Either way, the key is to keep returning to the feeling or attitude you wish to experience, until it is anchored in. Unlike that of the brain, the heart's intelligence will help you feel better quickly.

5. When you're out of touch with how you feel or when you're angry, hurt, frightened, or depressed, but don't know why, employ the wisdom of the heart. While breathing through the heart, ask it for clarity, "How do I feel?" Or "What's really bothering me?" This is a completely different experience than trying to think through what's going on with you, as you will see.

6. Whenever you feel out of balance in any way, mentally, emotionally, physically, or spiritually, breathe through the heart and ask your heart what it would take to bring your system back into balance. It might be a shift in attitude or an action called for, but your heart will tell you what is required. If you don't receive an answer right away, don't worry. Remain open, and it will eventually come.

7. When you're feeling happy, grateful, appreciative, loving, etc., it's a great practice to anchor those feelings and attitudes into your system by, you guessed it, breathing them into the heart. This builds your positive energy bank account for future use.

SIXTEEN

Grounding,
Shielding, and Clearing

We are blessed to now have access to so many wonderful grounding, shielding, and energy clearing techniques. Not long ago, only small pockets of the population had access to these practices, but today anyone who is interested in doing energy work can experiment with various techniques, many of which are quite simple and effective. If it's energy, you can change it, and everything's just energy. This shift in perspective makes all things possible.

The following are the energy "tricks" that I've personally found to be the most helpful and beneficial. They are quick and straightforward, which makes them easy to apply virtually any time and anywhere. Feel free to read through them briefly now, and then come back later to experiment with what works for you. As always, keep what works for you and don't worry about the rest. Note that several of the techniques in this and

175

the following chapter are modifications of the energy work of Amorah Quan Yin.[1]

Getting Grounded

Since we came here to reside in bodies, it is important to do any work from a base of groundedness. When we're ungrounded, we tend to space out easily, have trouble focusing, and may even become accident-prone because we're not present to steer our ship. When we're not steering our own ship, we become vulnerable to someone or something else taking the helm.

A basic grounding practice involves visualizing a grounding *cord* running from your energy body down into the crystalline core of the earth. Since Mother Earth has her own healing work to do, we don't want to attach directly into the ground, but all the way down to the energetic core, which is a transmutational field, a purifying force that allows us to release what we don't need without overtaxing the earth.

You can visualize your grounding cord as an 8" diameter beam of colored light, a silver cable, a treelike root, or whatever image works for you. The more substantial the cord, the more grounded you will feel. One day you might like the effect of a thin, sparkly tether that allows you plenty of freedom, whereas the next day you might require a tree trunk just to keep your feet on the ground.

Traditionally the grounding cord was run from the first chakra (at the base of the spine) down into the earth, but as we have evolved spiritually, many teachers have suggested that we ground from the second, fourth, or higher chakras, depending on our present focus. Please experiment and follow your own guidance regarding what type of grounding cord to visualize and which chakra to start from. There's no one right way to do this.

While insufficient grounding can cause you to feel like a kite in a windstorm, too much grounding can tie you down and prevent you from moving forward, so try out different cord types and see how they feel. Experiment also with different colors and see what effect these have on you personally. For example, a cord of royal blue light might help you feel strong and confident, while yellow energizes you.

When you begin your grounding practice, you may find that you need to replace your cord often to keep it fresh and effective. In the morning and before you go to sleep, visualize gently detaching your old grounding cord and releasing it into the core of the earth. Then create and send down a new cord based on your current needs or focus.

To complete the *circuit* of heaven and earth, run an etheric cord from your heart or other chakra up, up, up until it meets a bright star, which represents your energetic interface with God. Feel that energy traveling down the cord and entering your body through the top of your head. Now you are tethered to both earth and source energies.

Shielding and Healthy Boundaries

While there are no hard and fast rules to energy work, it is highly advised that you apply some form of psychic protection whenever you open yourself up energetically. While it may sound inconvenient or even paranoid, it's not a bad idea to shield yourself from outside interference even before getting out of bed in the morning.

If you've ever awakened feeling optimistic and refreshed only to find yourself upset and tense fifteen minutes later, following an interaction with a disgruntled spouse or child, you know how vulnerable your energy field can be. It's not that you want to block other people out; you just want to maintain your own "space" for the highest good of everyone involved.

In order to address the issue of healthy boundaries, let's begin with an explanation of *auras*, which are energy fields that radiate around the physical body. We each have a personal aura that is created by the processing of energy in the chakras, and each chakra contributes to the structure and maintenance of the auric field. When your chakras are balanced and functioning well, you have a strong, healthy, vibrant aura. Conversely, when your chakras are sluggish, damaged, etc., your aura will appear weak and dull.

A person with overly rigid boundaries will present with a contracted aura, extending perhaps only a few inches from her body. This can cause her to feel even more tense, separate, and vulnerable. At the other extreme is a person with overly loose boundaries, whose aura extends from several feet to a half-mile radius from his body. An overextended aura can cause spaciness and a tendency to feel and absorb other people's thoughts and emotions, which can be overwhelming.

Generally speaking, a good example of a healthy aura might appear egg-shaped and extend one and a half to three feet from the body in every direction. This is especially advisable in public situations; however, you may wish to extend your boundaries while in private or while connecting with nature, etc.

To observe and work with your auric field, close your eyes and start to get a sense of your aura. Don't worry if you can't see or feel anything; just relax and imagine a field of energy or light around you. By visualizing and applying your intention, adjust it so that it appears vibrant and strong and extends 18" to three feet away from your body in all directions, including below your feet. Notice how it feels as you make these adjustments. Do you feel safer, more vulnerable, more confined? This exercise is just a starting point. Feel free to continue adjusting until you find what works best for you.

Next, visualize a layer of golden light surrounding your egg-shaped, auric field. You may think of it as the light of the sun or as golden light of Christ-consciousness. This contributes to the overall strength and health of your aura and fills in any holes or rough edges. If you wish, you may add another layer of light around that. For instance, violet light (also known as the violet flame of transmutation) transforms and purifies negative energies that might try to permeate your energy field, while pink light tends to filter and soften the effects of outside energies.

When you're first starting out, as with the grounding exercise, it's a good idea to adjust and shield your aura in the morning as well as before you go to sleep at night. You can also shield your home or other environment from outside influences by doing the following exercise.

First, visualize a grounding cord of light extending from the ground level of the space down to the center of the earth. Next, imagine a two-foot diameter golden sun in the center of the space. Expand the golden sun slowly until it surrounds the entire space. Finally, surround the golden sun with a dome of violet light.

Likewise, you can shield your loved ones, car, or anything by visualizing divine golden light, or another color, around them. Save the intense protective white light for more extreme situations, as this can stifle one's ability to be fully present and engaged. I also like to affirm that Archangel Michael and his legion of protector angels are present to keep my loved ones safe, especially while riding in a car.

In fact, you can apply this aid to anyone, anytime. If you see or hear about someone struggling, challenged, or in pain, feel free to put light and/or angels around them. If they need healing, you might visualize green light and call in Archangel Raphael or Jesus, both of whom are excellent healers and comforters. When you extend this sort of love to others, you will find that the blessings are returned to you manifold.

When applying these energy techniques to others, should you worry about interfering with their free will? This is an important question to consider because it is possible to adversely affect people's energy fields without meaning to. For instance, if you are deathly afraid that something will happen to your child, and you apply multiple layers of physical and psychic protection to him, he is likely to either take on your fear or feel smothered by all that "protection." (Remember the television commercial where the little boy is engulfed in bubble wrap?)

This is why healthy boundaries and spiritual work are so important. Your job is to tend to your own space and not barge into that of other people. If you have children, your role is to provide a safe-enough, healthy-enough, and loving-enough environment for them to grow up in, but not to control their every move. You cannot "protect" them from what they signed up to experience. Once you realize this and accept it on some level, it allows you to pull your hooks out of people, surround them with loving (not fearful) energy, and send them on their way, knowing that this is in everybody's best interest.

A basic rule of thumb regarding doing energy work on others is that you approach it with only the highest good of the other person in mind. Any form of fear, control, or manipulation that you exert, even unconsciously, will tend to boomerang back on you, so it pays to be conscientious with regard to your intentions and practices.

It's also true that people's energy systems are equipped to reject a great deal of outside influence. This means, for instance, that your mother can turn away the angels or healing light if she chooses to experience suffering, which might be appropriate given the lesson she came to learn. This often happens outside of people's conscious awareness. So feel free to send love and support, knowing that if the recipient wants it she will get it, and if she doesn't want it, it will be returned to you.

Energy Clearing

As human beings who are designed to be susceptible to the effects of our environment and other people, the issue of energy clearing is of paramount importance. The more sensitive you are, the more readily you will pick up and absorb energies from places, people, or other entities that don't belong to you and do not serve you. You might even willingly take on certain people's problems in a misguided attempt to alleviate their suffering. We are also prone to building up our own negativity, anger, and fear, so add all of that potentially troublesome energy together, and it's easy to see why we fall prey to illness, anxiety, depression, addictions, etc.

Regardless of how it happens, even those of us with healthy boundaries can accumulate unhealthy energies that need to be cleared away on a regular basis. We've already discussed some of the functional ways people naturally do this, such as having a good cry, exercising, journaling, or talking to a friend—as well as some of the dysfunctional and ineffective ways people try to eradicate negative thoughts and feelings, such as engaging in obsessive, compulsive, or reckless behavior.

In this section, we will go over a number of simple energy clearing ideas and practices that have proven to be effective for many people. Some people use the same one or two techniques over and over again, while others prefer to have a larger repertoire to choose from, depending on the situation.

For instance, when I'm feeling flooded with negative or fearful thoughts the first thing I do is pray, "God, I surrender ALL of this to you, NOW," and I visualize all the thoughts and feelings moving up out of my energy field and into the light of God. This usually has an immediate calming effect. On the other hand, when I'm feeling negativity gradually building, I'm more likely to call in the violet flame to surround me and help burn away everything that is not mine or does not serve me. This takes longer and is subtler, but is highly effective.

The following discussion is meant as an introduction to the wonderful world of energy clearing. We'll start by highlighting basic, but important, concepts and practices that will help you release unwanted energy and *maintain* that improved state. Then, in the next chapter, we will go over several visualization techniques that experienced energy workers love to use for daily energy clearing, as well as healing deep and persistent issues.

Self-Expression

One of the most fundamental and helpful ways of clearing built-up energy is to express it or put it outside of yourself. Ideally this is done in a way that does not cause problems for yourself or anyone else. For instance, venting your authentic feelings in a therapy session may help you release toxic energy, while at the same time providing the therapist with valuable information about who you are and how she can best serve you. On the other hand, venting the same feelings to a different person in a different situation can amount to *dumping* and can cause overwhelm, hurt feelings, anger, guilt, etc. You've probably experienced both sides of this equation and know how destructive expressing one's feelings can be if done insensitively.

Luckily there are many great ways to express and release unwanted feelings or energy that won't get you into trouble. As previously discussed, *journaling* is not only an effective way of identifying issues, sorting things out, and working through difficult thoughts and emotions, but it is one of the best ways I've experienced for spewing negativity. You can rant and rave all you like on the page; you can call names, use profanity, blame others for your problems, and generally behave badly, if that's what you need to do.

Sometimes you may start out looking like Mozart in a 2:00 a.m. music-writing frenzy, like you can't get it on paper fast enough. Then what happens is miraculous. As the negativity drains out of you, you gradually slow down, regain composure, and might even start feeling a little guilty for what you wrote. This is okay. Let it go. If you were very upset, it needed to be expressed, and writing it out served you well. Now you're ready to talk to your teenager about hosting that "kegger" while you were out of town.

Depending on your temperament and other factors, your style of expressing and releasing unwanted energy will vary. For instance, your idea of venting may be subtle compared to the previous scenario. If, however, you're not comfortable with the idea of ranting in any form, you may be bumping up against ego control issues that hold beliefs such as, "You're above those petty emotions," "Spiritual people don't say things like that," or "If you acknowledge those feelings, they will consume you."

Many spiritually aware people walk around constantly reciting *affirmations* and never admit to a negative thought. While affirmations and focusing on the positive are valuable practices, they can backfire if they cause you to *repress* unhealthy energy. Authenticity requires us to first acknowledge energies that do not serve us. Avoiding and feeling threatened by our humanness does not make it go away.

There will come a time in your spiritual evolution when your vibration will be so consistently high that you will no longer accumulate negative energy. Until then, however, we benefit most by being courageous enough to face where we really are and clearing negative energies on a regular basis. If that sometimes requires scribbling a four-letter word or stomping a foot, so be it. We need not judge that.

Sometimes it is important to express or communicate your thoughts or feelings directly to another person in order to release unwanted energy or remedy a situation. This can be done passively, assertively, or aggressively. Passive and/or aggressive communication styles are not considered ideal and can cause a host of personal and interpersonal problems.

Assertive, nondefensive, or nonviolent communication styles, on the other hand, allow you to express yourself honestly, cleanly, and respectfully, while caring about the recipient's feelings. While these styles of communication make your life much easier, they do not necessarily guarantee a pleasant conversation, because sometimes what you have to say will not be received well no matter how carefully you express it. Even so, expressing yourself honestly when necessary is critical to your well-being and the well-being of your relationships.

For most of us, this requires making fundamental changes to our communication style as well as a lot of practice, but it can be done, and the rewards are fantastic. There are many great resources available to help you and your loved ones learn to communicate lovingly and effectively.

In addition to journaling and communicating with others well, there are a multitude of other positive ways to express oneself and release unwanted energy and stress. These are highly individual and include everything from dancing to painting to singing to collecting coins, and beyond. If it gets your authentic life force energy circulating, it will serve as an energy clearing practice. As we discussed before, being passionate about something means that it is part of your purpose for being here; therefore following and expressing that bliss will raise your vibration and make you feel lighter.

Connecting with Nature

Fresh air and trees naturally provide humans with oxygen to breathe; fire and sun sustain us with warmth; the earth and her creatures produce food for us to eat; and rain cleanses and provides us with water to drink. We came to this gorgeous, diverse, and bountiful planet because it was perfectly suited for our desired human experience, and its exquisiteness drew souls to want to return here time and time again.

Sadly perhaps, as time has passed, humanity has become further and further removed from the very nature that we ventured here to experience. Whereas we used to rise and set with the sun and breathe fresh air all day long, most of us now live independent of the signals of nature. Some of us spend our days and nights in sealed buildings and rarely even go outdoors. The industrial age mentality that brought about an objectification of the earth is something that we are only now beginning to awaken from.

Because we are part of the earth and the earth is part of us, this damaged connection has caused great suffering on both sides of the relationship. The planet has been unconscionably abused, and many of us humans have lost track of one of our greatest energy clearing and balancing allies, which is nature.

What's so great about the great outdoors? It's *alive*. If you've ever eaten a peach off the tree or a tomato off the vine, you know the difference between a substance that is full of life force energy and one that is not. Likewise, the woods, the mountains, the oceans, even the deserts are alive in a way that city skyscrapers are not.

Luckily for us, nature is not an all-or-nothing proposition. Bringing animals, trees, plants, stones or crystals, fountains, etc., into an environment can transform it substantially. Curling up in front of a crackling fire, soaking in a warm bath, or tending to beloved pets or plants can bring us great peace and serve as effective energy-clearing resources.

Gardening, eating a meal outside, relaxing on the patio, or enjoying a sunset can be restorative. Likewise, walks in your urban or suburban neighborhood, providing you feel safe and the air quality is adequate, can serve as a reasonable substitute for an invigorating nature hike.

The trick is in assessing your nature needs and making changes to your routine or lifestyle that would help you feel more clear and balanced. For instance, some people must live near the ocean or they feel like fish out of water, while others are perfectly happy, even at home, living in the hustle and bustle of big city life. Some people could not imagine life without their cats and dogs, while others thrive most on being surrounded with green plants and blue skies. Some people love physical work outdoors, while others are content with intellectual work done in a comfortable, controlled environment.

If you are a farm boy at heart, you may feel suffocated working in an office or living in the suburbs. Likewise, if you are a fair weather girl, you might experience chronic depression living in a cold or rainy climate. Take a moment to evaluate your work and living situations. Are they in alignment with who you are? If not, you might be suffering and building stress and resentment needlessly. Regardless of your preferences, you might benefit from consciously experimenting with new, different, and/or *more* experiences with nature and its elements.

Shaking It Off

There are many ways in which we intuitively release energies that we don't want or need. For instance, following an upset on the soccer field, a coach will remind a player to "brush it off" or "shake it off." Right before a performance or race, many athletes can be observed focusing and shaking out their arms, legs, etc. They do this instinctively, because it loosens them up, releases nervousness, and allows them to perform at their best. And it's common knowledge that taking a deep breath and sighing or blowing out deeply is a great way to calm down and relieve stress.

In fact, many effective stress-reduction techniques involve centering and shaking tension off in some form or another, be it physical exercise or some other type of movement. People who exercise on a regular basis realize the profound energy clearing benefits that it holds. Dancers, of course, make this an art form.

There are also many ways that our bodies release tension that can be outside of our control and in some cases disturbing. For instance, children who have not yet learned how to regulate their energy input can melt down or exhibit tantrum behavior when they've had all they can take. This typically consists of foot stomping, crying, screaming, hitting, and possibly the stereotypical lying down and pounding fists and feet into the floor. This can be upsetting for everyone involved.

Among the adult set, some of the same behaviors can occur, but also prevalent are such involuntary actions as foot tapping, pacing, hand wringing, yelling, cursing, nail biting, finger tapping, skin picking, teeth grinding, nervous tics, twitches, and more. Needless to say, these can be embarrassing and unsettling, and the compulsive quality of many of these physical behaviors would indicate the body's desperate need to discharge built-up energy.

In order to avoid this energy buildup, a psychotherapist friend of mine used to deliberately flick her fingers, as if to get water off, when a client told her something disturbing. She said that this was her way of quickly dispelling the energy before it had a chance to soak in. Occasionally, a client would feel rejected by this, and the therapist would take the opportunity to explain how it is never appropriate for a person to willingly absorb the negative energy of another. It's entirely unnecessary and is often harmful to the person on the receiving end. However, many well-intended people make a career of absorbing other people's pain.

A dramatic example of this occurred for me several years ago when I was in relationship with someone who had a particular issue that was getting in the way of our friendship. It was an issue that I had never struggled with personally, and I remember thinking, "Gee, if I could relieve my friend of this issue, I'm sure I could quickly heal it, and then we would both be happy."

What I didn't realize was that my willingness to shoulder this burden led somehow to an *unconscious* agreement or contract being forged between the two of us. All I knew consciously was that within a few months I *owned* that issue outright. I didn't even know what had hit me. Looking back, it was as if I'd made a proverbial "deal with the devil." The cruel irony was that my friend, who now felt magically free of the issue, started blaming me for having it, because it was getting in the way of our friendship!

It was years before I realized what had happened and several more years before I figured out how to release and transmute that constellation of unhealthy energy. I later realized that the primary reason I'd had so much trouble healing that issue was that it had not been my issue to heal. *My* issue was that I was a rescuer with poor boundaries. I suppose the debacle led to success in the long run (and I do mean "long"), because it taught me to mind my own psychic business.

The great news is that we can be loving, caring friends, parents, or facilitators without having to sacrifice ourselves. God, or source energy, is expertly equipped to absorb and recycle any and all negative or unhealed energy that we may need to release. Unlike us, God does not suffer in doing so; therefore, you need never worry that you're dumping on God. This is why *surrender* in the twelve-step program model works so well. We take all of that fear and shame and confusion and addiction, and we say, "God, *you* take this, because it's more than I can handle right now!" And when you're really ready to let it go, it's *gone*.

So experiment with *positive* ways of shaking off unwanted energy as it comes in. This requires that you stay alert to how you feel. For instance, if you feel fine one moment and the next moment you're upset because of something experienced or subtly felt, take a moment to gather up that energy with your intention or breath and release it with a sigh, a few flicks of the hands, a run around the block, a prayer of surrender, or whatever feels right to you. Nipping it in the bud will save you much discomfort (and potential disease) down the road.

SEVENTEEN

Visualizations for Releasing
and Healing

We have previously discussed several exercises that serve the purposes of creating/manifesting or shielding/protecting, as well as the technique of chakra spinning, which is a powerful energy balancing and clearing practice.

In addition to these "basic wardrobe pieces," we have access to many other simple energy work practices that involve a visualization infused with intention. Don't worry if you have trouble forming a visual picture. Simply imagine or hold that the picture is there, in the same way that you would hold anything in mind that you cannot see in front of you.

The Etheric Rose

The term "blowing roses" refers to an energy clearing practice done using etheric roses and is purported to date back several centuries. The rose is considered to be one of the highest vibrating plants on the earth, as well as an ancient symbol of purity and healing. As an archetype of such, the rose holds the power to extract energies in our field that are of an impure or foreign nature. The etheric rose absorbs the unwanted energies and is then sent away from us to dissolve or explode, thus transmuting the impure energy into pure life force energy.

There are various ways to employ the use of roses. You can either place the rose inside your energy field, at the site of the mental, emotional, or physical disturbance (in the center of your head, solar plexus, heart, etc.) for the purpose of absorbing the energy like a sponge; or you can place the rose outside of your aura to act as a large energy magnet. Either way, it is critical that you *release* the rose well away from your own or anyone else's energy field, so that it doesn't get lodged somewhere before it has transmuted the troublesome energy. (I like to imagine the rose drifting up out of the earth's atmosphere and then exploding like fireworks on the fourth of July, but if you prefer something subtler, a simple "poof" will do.)

This technique can be used for clearing virtually any unwanted energy, be it someone else's issue or energetic influence that you have taken on, a fear or phobia, judgments, faulty beliefs, "perfect" pictures (that you compare yourself to), general stress, anxiety, anger, jealousy, etc., and is most effective when done while experiencing the feelings acutely.

After closing your eyes and grounding yourself, visualize a fully blooming rose of any color and size you desire. Check in with yourself about the best placement of the rose, and go ahead and position it there. If it's helpful you can imagine a picture, word, or other representation of that which is to be released in the rose itself.

Next, see or feel the rose begin to absorb or pull out the unwanted energy. Watch it for at least thirty seconds. As it absorbs difficult energies, you may see it begin to close up, shrivel, or start to drop petals. When this happens, it's time to remove the rose from your energy field and blow it up.

Now notice how you feel. You may need to create and blow up several roses before you feel complete in the clearing process. If the issue or energy is intense, long standing, or otherwise persistent, you may need to chip away at it over time. Some issues heal a little at a time and are like peeling away an onion in layers. Big clearing all at once can be extremely disruptive (as in the "kundalini" experience), so more often than not release happens in stages. Be patient and know that your intentions and efforts are never really wasted.

If the rose you are blowing represents someone else's energy, influence, or pictures (of who or how you should be), and you feel guilty about rejecting or disposing of it, don't worry. That person's energy is being transmuted or cleaned up and then returned to him. What he does with it from there, of course, is up to him. The important thing is that if it is not yours and it does not serve you, then it's appropriate to let it go.

The Violet Flame

Just as rays of sunlight passing through a prism break down into the seven colors of the rainbow, so does spiritual light refract into seven rays. These rays each carry a particular color, frequency, and aspect of divine consciousness. It is believed that fairly recently the ascended master Saint Germain provided humanity access to the violet flame, where it had previously been denied, for the purpose of ushering in a new era of peace and enlightenment.

Author Elizabeth Clare Prophet writes, "The violet ray is known as the seventh ray. When you invoke it in the name of God, it descends as a beam of spiritual energy and bursts into a spiritual flame in your heart as the qualities of mercy, forgiveness, justice, freedom and transmutation."[1] This violet flame is known as a powerful solvent of negative energy, karma, etc., and can be used as an energetic shield as well as a furnace that burns away unwanted psychic residue. Like the practice of blowing roses, the violet flame does not destroy, per se, but transmutes and recycles the negative into positive.

Using the violet flame is quite straightforward. I like to ground myself first and seal my aura with protective golden white light or call in Archangel Michael to supervise the session. The reason for this is that, paradoxically, sometimes calling forth *more* light can actually attract *more* dark energy, like a porch light attracts moths. Not to worry, just apply a little protection and then visualize yourself, your home, your city, etc., surrounded and enfolded in violet light.

Elizabeth Clare Prophet likes to accompany this visualization with a *decree*, also delivered by Saint Germain, which states, "I AM a Being of Violet Fire. I AM the purity God desires." This, she believes, is important in locking in our intention and amplifying the purifying effects of the violet flame, but it is optional. As always, feel free to experiment and decide what works best for you.

The violet flame may feel warm and energetic to you, cool and invigorating, or like nothing at all. Imagine that it is cleansing, dissolving, or burning away that which you desire to be free of. This can be done anytime, anywhere, and for any function. Some people apply the violet flame as if it's one of those all-purpose cleaners advertised on television. They spray a little here, spray a little there. Others approach it as they would a sacred ritual. Experiment with it and you will find what works for you, but start slowly, because it can be very powerful. The first time you use it you might remain inside the violet flame for only a minute or two.

The violet flame can be part of your daily meditation. It can be a clearing practice done at the end of the day to remove psychic debris or any other unwanted energy. It can be used to clear karma by concentrating on the issue or karmic relationship and surrounding it in the violet flame. It can be used for physical healing, as well as mental, emotional, and spiritual healing. You can even use it as a buffer when you know you will be encountering someone or something that tends to affect you adversely. This, in fact, is a service, as it transmutes and upgrades the other party's energy even as it protects your own field.

If you feel like you need to cleanse and refresh your field and you only have a few minutes, try the following violet flame meditation.

1. Get in a comfortable position, close your eyes, and breathe several times in and out of the heart area.
2. From the heart, send down a grounding cord to the crystalline core of the earth. Once connected, breathe

that pure energy up the cord and out the crown chakra at the top of your head, letting it cascade down around your body.

3. Next, visualize a rain shower of divine golden liquid light, bathing and cleansing your aura. Let it rain for at least a couple minutes.

4. Finally, surround and enfold your entire auric field with the violet flame, allowing it to burn for a minute or two. Feel it burn away the last vestiges of psychic debris. Remove the violet flame, and open your eyes.

Removing Cords

Psychic or etheric cords may appear as tube-like structures that run from one person's chakra system to another's. They are used for the purpose of energy exchange. There are beneficial, love-based cords, such as between mother and baby and between healthy friends and lovers, and although cords can be used for positive sharing, they are often the result of fear-based attachment, codependency, unforgiveness, or even attempts to control or manipulate another. You may be entirely unaware of cords you have received from, or given to, others. Etheric cords are a significant source of energy draining and contamination.

For instance, if a person to whom you are connected is experiencing a life challenge or becomes depressed, needy, etc., he will unconsciously siphon your energy via the etheric cord. You may become depressed, exhausted, or even ill for no apparent reason.

We most often form etheric cords with our parents, children, siblings, spouses, ex-spouses, lovers, ex-lovers, close friends, and even homes. Generally, conflictual relationships attach at your solar plexus; love-based relationships or those with grief attach at your heart chakra; burdensome relationships attach at your shoulders or neck; and sexual relationships attach at your sacral chakra. In fact, some people are still corded, unconsciously, with many former lovers, which may not do wonders for their current relationship![2]

In order to feel great and move forward spiritually, it's important to release any cords of fear that may be attached to you. This does not mean that you are rejecting or abandoning anyone, but rather that you are reclaiming your own energy and allowing others to do the same. It means releasing the *dysfunctional* part of the relationship. Of course, any mutually beneficial cords may stay, but those that do not serve you ultimately do not serve others and should be let go.

Sometimes when we discover that someone has been siphoning our energy or trying to control or manipulate us by way of a cord, the first instinct is to get rid of the cord as quickly as possible, even in a hostile manner. While it's understandable to feel this way, it's important to remove the cord with care. This is because tearing a cord out can actually damage your chakra and can cause the other person to react or even lash out psychically. Likewise, attempting to unceremoniously cut cords can result in desperate attempts by the other person to re-cord with you. Therefore, removing cords should be done skillfully and with the utmost care. Once you are free of dysfunctional cords, you will gradually learn to sense new cords that come in, and you can more easily manage or remove them as you go along.

There are multiple ways to remove etheric cords, and some are more effective than others. As usual, intention is key in helping to identify and remove cords. If you relax, close your eyes, take a few deep breaths, and ground yourself, you can start to get a sense of where you might have cords attached to you. If you run your hand through your energy field near your body in all directions, you may start to feel variations in energy. You might feel hot spots or areas that feel tingly or dense. When you notice something, slowly run your hand forward toward the front of your aura. If it is a cord, the tube-like energy will seem to extend to the edge of your aura and will not dissipate.

When you have located a potential cord, see if you get a sense of whom it is attached to, or ask your guidance for a name. It might be obvious to you, or you might be surprised to discover that it belongs to someone you have not seen or heard from in years.

Next, return to the place where the cord attaches to your body. Visualize this spot bathed in divine golden light. Using your hand, ever so gently loosen the cord around the edges until it detaches from your body. Place the end of the cord in an etheric rose, and then send the two up, well out of your aura, and blow them up. Continue visualizing golden healing light filling the spot where the cord was removed.

You can repeat this process for locating and removing other cords, especially those that extend from the front of your body. For those that protrude from the back of your body, as is often the case with sneakier or more covert cords, you may need to project an image of your backside just in front of you. Run your hand over this image with the intention of locating cords. When you find a cord, remove it in the same way as described above.

You might also detect evidence of psychic attacks, especially in the back. This can happen when we are unprotected and someone consciously or unconsciously hurls anger at us. It might manifest as an energetic dagger, arrow, fireball, etc., that becomes lodged in the energy body. You can remove and dispose of these in the same way as the cords.

If all this seems too abstract or you find that you're unable to detect anything in your field, don't worry. There are other ways to identify and remove etheric cords, but they rely on the help of others. The first way is to find a good energy worker who is experienced in doing this kind of work. The other way is to enlist the help of a spirit helper such as Archangel Michael.

Archangel Michael is a great ally and hands-on helper in the area of energy clearing. His primary function here on earth is to clear away dark or dense energy, and he is depicted carrying a sword, which he uses to defend and protect us from negative outside influences. He does this for the planet, and he does this for us individually, if we ask.

To elicit the help of Archangel Michael, prepare yourself as you would for any meditative experience. Mentally call on him, and ask him to remove all cords that do not serve you. Allow some time, and pay attention to whatever feelings, sensations, or messages you might receive. For instance, you might become aware of your heart area, while remembering your first boyfriend or you might feel a sensation in your shoulder and see a picture of your mother nagging you. This information will help you understand what cords have been affecting you and what work might be necessary to prevent re-cording.

When you sense that Archangel Michael has completed his work, make sure to call in the golden healing light to bathe and act as a salve for all the spots in your aura where cords have been removed. Thank Archangel Michael for his assistance.

A Word about Addictions and Compulsions

Previously we discussed the human tendency to distract and medicate ourselves from our anxiety and pain by employing the use of food, alcohol, drugs, or some other obsessive or compulsive behavior. These struggles can go on year after year and get us nowhere. If you find yourself in that pattern, it is important to do whatever is necessary to break the cycle. It may mean going to therapy, joining a twelve-step program, or finding the right information that affects a shift in you.

For example, if you're a compulsive overeater and you've been yo-yo dieting for five, ten, twenty, or thirty years, it's time to try something different. There are wonderful books, such as *Intuitive Eating* by Evelyn Tribole and Elyse Resch, that can help you make friends with your body as well as face and effectively deal with the reasons for the overeating. There are similar resources available for virtually any addictive pattern, so please consider looking into them.

Another important factor to consider is that we may have inadvertently attracted low-vibrating entities or dark energies that feed off of addictions and altered states. When we "check out," they check in. To separate yourself from these energies, you can use many of the processes outlined in this book and others for clearing and releasing; you can find a practitioner who specializes in this kind of energy work; and/or you can learn to consciously choose the light whenever you feel addictive energies trying to pull you off course. A friend of mine likes to say, "I acknowledge you, dark brother, but I *choose* the light." This is a powerful affirmation, because it demonstrates that we know what's going on, we know we have a choice, and we consciously choose our highest good.

EIGHTEEN

Advanced Steps to Awakening
and Ascension

B y now you have begun the process of embracing life in the present moment, making peace with who you are and who you are not, getting acquainted with your various subpersonalities, and releasing fear and psychic debris. Soon you will be ready to move on to the following exercises/levels in the conscious spiritual awakening process. Even though the path can be naturally self-guiding and some-times require no conscious action on your part, it's helpful to know what you're moving toward, so that you can relax and nurture that budding sense of true self.

Please note that this series of steps is but one of many formulas for assisting the awakening process. Virtually every spiritual system and religion has its own recipe for spiritual advancement. Depending on any number of factors, such as your cultural background, previous religious experience or lack thereof, worldview, personality, etc., you will find yourself attracted to some methods, while repelled by others.

For instance, someone raised in the Catholic Church might not relate to the evocative dancing or drumming rituals of an indigenous tribe. Likewise, someone who approaches life emotionally might not be attracted to a cognitive presentation of spiritual evolution. Words almost always fall short of experience, especially the closer to spirit we become, but they can pave the way to the next level of experience. When you are truly ready to move forward on your path, that path will be laid out for you. All you have to do is pay attention.

Step One: Experiencing Your Inner Sanctuary

If you haven't done so previously, create an inner sanctuary for yourself. This is done by imagining or visualizing a peaceful, beautiful place within your heart or at the center of your head (behind your third eye) that is all your own. It can appear as a private place in nature, an ideal room or chamber, an enchanted garden, or whatever eases you into a feeling of safety and happiness. This sanctuary exists within you, not without.

Your sanctuary may change or evolve over time, so don't feel that you need to commit to any particular scene. Just begin by relaxing and asking yourself what type of space would work best for you today, and see what pops in. If visualization is not your strong suit, don't force it; just relax and find a place inside yourself that feels good. You may experience sounds, fragrances, words, or just peaceful stillness.

Spend a few minutes each day, or whenever possible, sitting quietly in this sanctuary space. Perhaps begin by lighting a candle, saying a prayer, or imagining yourself surrounded by light. When meditating, it's always a good idea to apply some form of energetic protection from unwanted external influences.

Say hello to God or your Higher Self, and then focus on opening your heart. Breathe into your heart and out of your heart, and take a moment to get clear about where your consciousness is right *now*. Without going into details, acknowledge the truth about your current state. How do you feel? Is anything troubling you? Just for a moment *accept* and *allow* these thoughts and feelings to be. This simple act can free you to be truly present in the moment. It will also direct you to what emotional or cognitive work may serve you, such as forgiving, energy clearing, making amends, etc.

If you are more comfortable stating your truth in an affirmative manner you might think or say something like, "Even though I feel sad and lonely right now, I know that I am always surrounded by God's love." But do allow yourself a moment to actually feel the sadness and loneliness. That moment of honest acknowledgment will make a big difference in your process. Denial can be toxic and stifling, while the act of acceptance makes movement possible.

Surrender or release your thoughts and feelings to God and your Higher Self. Ask questions, and wait for answers to come. Make sure to keep your journal and a pen close by in case you want to dialogue with higher or lower aspects of self, record insights you receive, or explore any area further.

Step Two: Aligning with Higher Self

Once you've become accustomed to spending time in your inner sanctuary, surrendering concerns, and doing inner voice dialogue, it's now time to start consciously aligning with your Higher Self. At this level, you are not seeking advice or guidance from a wise, *distant* Self, but beginning the process of stepping into that role for yourself.

Your intention for meditation becomes living in the experience of Higher Self. You consciously elevate yourself to that level for the duration of the exercise, steeping yourself in and contemplating the qualities of the divine: love, peace, wholeness, etc. When the voices of the lower self inevitably pop up, you address them from the perspective of Higher Self, as a caring parent addresses the issues of a beloved child.

If you notice a particularly stubborn or persistent issue that resists love, you might want to set aside time to go fully into the depths of it, without trying to uplift it. This issue or unhappy subpersonality represents some aspect of essence that has not come into expression or been actualized. Ego will continue presenting the issue until the conflict is resolved.

For instance, someone who nurtures others, but does not nurture herself properly, might struggle for years with overeating. This compulsion is the ego's attempt to fill the void, and the resulting problems are a red flag that can point out the internal deficiency. Dieting is not the answer. Learning to nurture and honor Self is, and sometimes this requires us the go deeply into the problem to understand what is going on. *All problems are an expression of separation from God*, and with a loving Higher Self at the helm, these issues can finally be resolved.

A few years ago there was a popular saying, "WWJD?" or "What would Jesus do?" Whether or not you relate to Jesus, this question offers a wonderful spiritual exercise designed to put you in touch with your Higher Self, which shares the wisdom and clarity of all divine beings. If you wish, you may substitute in your favorite spiritual figure, someone whom you can really relate to—perhaps an ascended master or even a highly advanced spiritual teacher you know. When faced with a conflict between higher and lower self, you can ask yourself, "What would Abraham, Mother Mary, etc., do?" The spiritual figure becomes a temporary projection screen for your own Higher Self, and you are then able to see the situation through the eyes of spirit.

In this meditation exercise, you are being asked to do the same thing. Even though you may not be constantly living at the level of Higher Self, you do have access to its wisdom. That part of you has been activated, and now it's just a matter of practicing and integrating it on a deeper level than before. This shift in perspective, if only for a few minutes a day, has the power to change your perspective forever.

Once this shift in perspective has been experienced, it becomes surprisingly easy to begin applying it during the day. No doubt you've been acting from this place, on and off, for some time, but now you are conscious of the shift. You have progressed from "To Me" to "By Me" to "Through Me," and now you are dipping your toes in the magnificent waters of "As Me." This is an exciting development, but one that will most definitely cause any unintegrated ego issues or blocks in the emotional body to surface. Your ego will *love* thinking of itself "As God."

Not to worry, it is all part of the grand awakening and ascension process. At this stage, you are being asked to practice applying the higher qualities of spirit as often as possible during the day and to begin viewing lower self issues (anxiety, jealousy, lack, etc.) from the perspective of Higher Self whenever possible. If something bothers you, stop, take a deep breath, identify the issue as an aspect of ego, and consciously step into the role of Higher Self. The more you do this, the more peaceful you will become.

At this level, *spiritual ambition* can get in the way of progress. In graduate school, we called this "Spiritual Olympics," whereby we inadvertently competed in such events as "Right Action," "Right Language," "Right Diet," and "Buddha Consciousness." This, of course, is the ego at work once again and is amusingly ironic. When you find yourself feeling spiritually superior to anyone or anything, stop, identify where this is coming from, and release that thought. It does not serve you or anyone else.

Step Three: The Merging of Selves

In the previous step, you practiced the art of elevating yourself to Higher Self status and training your ego's subpersonalities to trust and surrender to this essential self. The success of this effort can be measured by your overall ease in life or lack thereof. If your ego is still struggling for power, it has not yet realized the benefit of surrendering to spirit. It's not yet trusting that Higher Self has "got its back."

This is to be expected. Remember that the ego's job is to ensure your survival, and it takes that responsibility seriously. When you, operating as Higher Self, honor that loyalty and commitment and work lovingly with the subpersonalities, the ego will eventually loosen its grip and learn to defer to the guidance of the

Higher Self. When this has been achieved, it will then be possible for the higher and lower aspects of self to merge as one.

During your long career as a soul incarnating as human being, it has been necessary for Higher Self to guide your life from a safe distance. If it had been merged with the lower aspects of self, it would have become tainted and lost its eagle's eye perspective. It would have been of little value as a navigator and guardian of self. However, as the lower self becomes healed and transformed, it becomes safe and beneficial for the higher and lower selves to merge and operate as one. This represents the marriage of heaven and earth and is a big evolutionary step. This is ascension consciousness.

It might take weeks, months, years, or lifetimes of preparation, but when you feel ready to take the plunge, consider creating a personal ceremony in which you invite yourself, as Higher Self, to join more fully with the rest of your earthly incarnation. It will still be in charge, but will now preside from within, and not from above. In reality, this *descension* of Higher Self is a gradual process that has probably already begun for you, but stating your intention to be fully merged can only help the process along.

This proposal may or may not be accepted right away, depending on the wisdom of your Higher Self, but rest assured that your wishes have been noted, and your desire for union will be honored at the right and perfect moment.

Step Four: The Shifting of Identity

Once the higher and lower aspects of self begin to merge, there is a profound recognition of the idea set forth in Joseph

Campbell's *Perennial Philosophy*,[1] which essentially says, "I am the guidance that has been guiding me." You are now Higher Self expressing through a human personality.

At this level of spiritual development, you begin to view the angels, ascended masters, galactic emissaries, and other divine beings as peers, instead of superiors. You realize that we all share the same source of truth and wisdom, and while you continue to respect and honor them greatly, you no longer defer to them in the same way. You occasionally seek their counsel and assistance as a doctor occasionally seeks the counsel and assistance of a good attorney or tax accountant. We all have our special talents, and we are all essential pieces of the universal whole. We are here to work together for the highest good of all.

In this step, while the ego and subpersonalities are still distinct forces, they are no longer fighting for survival. Having chosen to cooperate with spirit, they are beginning to experience the comfort of a peaceful life. Their closer relationship to spirit is gradually raising their vibration and transforming them. For example, when someone behaves inconsiderately toward you, instead of becoming offended, you may notice a refreshing absence of reaction, or perhaps even concern for that person. What used to upset you no longer does, at least not on a regular basis.

As long as you are living in a physical body, you are subject to occasional feelings of separation, anxiety, etc., but the constant presence of the Higher Self brings a new level of perspective to most situations. What once felt senseless and tragic, as in the case of a devastating natural disaster, now, more gently, evokes feelings of compassion for the sufferers.

You may want to send prayers and aid, but in your heart, you know that this event is serving a higher purpose and that nothing is random. You may not understand it, but you accept it.

In this step, the shift in identity, from internal follower to leader, becomes more consistent. Instead of asking your Higher Self for guidance, you are often operating *as* Higher Self, providing guidance to the subpersonalities as needed. You are developing a highly sensitive self-monitoring system, and when you detect internal distress or upset, you learn to address it immediately. Whereas once the ego might have seized control, now, as Higher Self, you have the power to nip the situation in the bud. You stop, breathe, and invite the wayward aspect of self to rejoin with you.

Returning to the present moment, journaling, visiting the meditative sanctuary, and employing energy clearing techniques will continue to serve as indispensible tools for maintaining a peaceful and functional self. The integration process involves ongoing management and education of subpersonalities. You've come a long way, but there's still work to be done.

Step Five: Mastering Presence

At this point *self*-maintenance becomes extremely important, because Higher Self will not reside in a chaotic space. Perhaps the best way to maintain internal stability in a difficult situation is to become proficient at recognizing and honoring what is going on for you at any given moment. As a human being, if you are always basking in the glow of spirit, you may not be as present in your body as you need to be, and you may miss the early signs and signals of distress, which eventually build up.

Whereas at previous levels you might have been unconsciously popping in and out of your body depending on inner and outer circumstances, you now find it easier to stay present in your body, no matter what is going on. As you move through the day, notice every internal signal of stress and immediately surrender that aspect of self to the light.

Experiment with how this works best for you. Then, one by one, each subpersonality becomes healed and integrated. Higher Self does not have baggage, and eventually neither will you. At this level of development, it will be much easier for you to maintain self than it was before, but making this a priority is more important than ever. Taking a moment for yourself is no longer a luxury, but a necessity, and by doing this, you serve not only yourself, but the entire universe.

Likewise, at this stage of development, it is of critical importance to be able to observe life and the world without indulging in judgment. Any judgment that goes beyond healthy discernment needs to be addressed and released. You have already learned to accept life on life's terms, released the urgency associated with time, and you no longer believe in injustice or tragedy, so the final act of mastering presence is *practicing*.

Step Six: Ascension Consciousness

Having mastered presence, you are now experiencing yourself and the world in a different way. The levels of self have merged, and lower energies have been transmuted, which is to say transformed or purified by source. There is virtually no internal commentary or conflict. You have constant access to the joyous, timeless world of spirit, and it is from here that you receive your guidance. This is a very different way of life.

Depending on your life contract, you may still be active in an exterior life purpose that requires you to stay grounded in your body and to maintain intellectual thought processes. You might be a spiritual teacher or leader of some sort. You might be a bodhisattva, a fully enlightened person who chooses to remain on earth to guide others.

You now possess a luminous quality, as your mind/body has reached a vibration so relatively high that your cells have released much of their density and are taking in more and more spiritual light. Energetically, ascension is defined as the transformation of matter into light, and this process is occurring for human beings, animals, and the earth herself, as we are all connected and part of the same system. The physical body takes on a more youthful and vibrant appearance.

While the entire spiritual evolution process is one of gradual ascension, when you achieve this status while still in a physical body, you have achieved an advanced state of earthly ascension. You are living heaven on earth.

While some contracts require a person to maintain a moderate to high level of centeredness in the body, another person at this level may appear to be drifting off into a world where such physical circumstances do not concern her. From the perspective of ego, this individual may appear "spaced out" or even mentally deficient, because she is no longer residing in the body/mind, but in the world of spirit. Instead of inviting spirit into the body, she has followed bliss up and out of the body. The life-force energy no longer strongly inhabits the physical body; thus the body experiences decline.

Attaining enlightenment while living in a physical body is a spiritual feat that represents graduation from the physical world. Whether or not it is of benefit to stay on in a particular body for the purpose of serving humanity depends on an individual's contract. It may be that she is of higher value serving from the other side of the veil or returning later in a different body, in which cases it would be perfectly reasonable to shed her current "earth suit" and move on. There's no right way to ascend, and spirit honors all choices.

For those who stay there is much work to be done to assist others in the global ascension process.

Step Seven: The Great Beyond

Although you might tend to think of spiritual enlightenment as being the ultimate goal, it is really just another step in the infinite journey of spirit. Once you have achieved ascension-consciousness, which may be characterized by a certain level of vibration and light saturation in the body/mind, all kinds of amazing things happen.

You are now, and perhaps have been for some time, plugged in *multidimensionally*, which is to say you have conscious contact not only in the third and fourth dimensions (the lower planes of existence), but also the fifth dimension and above. You might experience profound telepathy, clairvoyance, advanced powers of manifestation, avatar abilities, the ability to receive higher dimensional *languages of light*, etc. You might begin to think in terms of tones and geometries, for which there are no 3-D translations. The possibilities are endless and incomprehensible by the lower, limited mind.

Conclusion

While it is impossible to know what your experiences will be as you advance through these various levels of existence, know in your heart that all of the work you have done throughout time and space has been, and always will be, honored and celebrated. All of the times you made a choice of any kind, all the moments you suffered despair or rage, all the instances you doubted that there was a God, you were serving a truly heroic role in the expansion of the universe.

As you have probably noticed, the spiritual path, the evolutionary journey from spirit state into ego and back to spirit again is a long and winding road, often exhausting and sometimes perilous. Just when you think you have conquered a fear or achieved mastery over a problem area of your life, you find yourself careening off into a ditch, perhaps getting stuck in the mud or snow, or even sustaining injury.

Sometimes you are graced with moments of clarity, epiphanies that convince you that you will never see things the same as you did before; you will never fall into *that* trap again. Occasionally these experiences take hold, but more often they do not, and you find yourself in the frustrating and sometimes even devastating position of falling backward into an old pattern of low self-esteem, addiction, abuse, etc. This is particularly distressing because you know you had been gifted with a divine dispensation, only to seemingly lose it or throw it away.

Likewise, sometimes through great personal effort or a difficult life experience, you *learn* a powerful lesson. Perhaps, for example, you almost lose someone you love due to your neglect. This experience awakens you to intense love and appreciation for this person, and you vow to never take her for granted again. But then you take her for granted again, and the relationship ends.

These "mistakes," these human failings are what we came here to negotiate. When we blame others for our problems, we have missed the point entirely, but when we feel the effects of our errors and learn something from them, anything at all, we have made progress.

The perfectionist notion that says if we work hard enough, become good enough, we will get to take our place with God, be saved, or become worthy of love, is truly a trap set by the ego. As long as we are human, we will make mistakes and experience setbacks. There is no *once and for all*, and no "getting it right" *starting Monday*.

If you're like so many sincere fellow travelers, you will have learned this the hard way, but perhaps you will also have begun to realize that loving and honoring yourself, as much as possible and whenever possible, is what we really came here to do. Truly, this is one of the greatest contributions you can make to the universe.

This earth experience is a journey, not a destination. Even with our spiritual goals and ideals, even with all the talk of awakening and ascension, the truth is that from a Higher Self perspective, we're already exactly where we need to be. When we learn to love *more*, that will be exactly where we need to be.

Believe it or not, you, right this moment, are a bright light in the universe. Even with all your fears and all your shortcomings, you are a breathtakingly beautiful and courageous spark of the divine. When you can feel that in your heart, when you can appreciate your body just the way it is, and when you can sense the oneness of all of creation, you have remembered who you are. But don't worry if you forget again; it's all part of the journey.

So go forth, intrepid traveler, knowing that you have the support of the entire universe behind you. Do what makes your heart sing, choose love and forgiveness whenever possible, follow your own guidance, and remember to breathe. Everything is in divine order, and everything's going to turn out just fine. There's no race and no finish line. This is a hero's *journey,* and you, dear friend, are a hero.

Endnotes

Chapter 1

1. Eckhart Tolle, *A New Earth: Awakening to Your Life's Purpose* (New York: Dutton, 2005), 259.
2. Barbara Marx Hubbard, *Emergence: The Shift from Ego to Essence* (Newburyport: Hampton Roads Publishing, 2001), 4.
3. Lee Carroll, "The Eight Shifts of Enlightenment," *Kryon Channelling* (April 8, 2008), http://www.kryon.com_channel107_mexico_01.html, fourth shift.
4. Amorah Quan Yin, *The Pleiadian Workbook: Awakening Your Divine Ka* (Santa Fe: Bear and Company, Inc., 1996), 36-37.

Chapter 2

1. Steve Rother, *Re-member: A Handbook for Human Evolution* (Las Vegas: Lightworker, 2005), 16-18.
2. Joseph Campbell, *The Hero's Journey: Joseph Campbell on His Life and Work,* ed. Phil Cousineau (San Francisco: Harper and Row Publishers, 1990), xv.

Chapter 3

1. Karen Linsley, "Stages of Spiritual Development," *Lake Tahoe New Thought Examiner* (April 8, 2010), http://www.examiner.com/x-23382-Lake-Tahoe-New-Examiner~y2010m3d5-Stag.
2. Hubbard, *Emergence*, 185.
3. Ibid., 190.
4. Carroll, "The Eight Shifts of Enlightenment," seventh shift.

Chapter 4
1. Foundation for Inner Peace, ed., *A Course in Miracles* (Glen Ellen: Foundation for Inner Peace, 1985). Note that there are several good interpretations available including: *A Return to Love: Reflection on the Principles of A Course in Miracles,* by Marianne Williamson.
2. Esther and Jerry Hicks, *Ask and It Is Given: Learning to Manifest Your Dreams* (Carlsbad, CA: Hay House, 2004), 114.

Chapter 5
1. Tashira Tachi-ren, *What Is Lightbody?* (Lithia Springs: World Tree Press, 2007), 79.
2. Tolle, *A New Earth,* 206-208.
3. Ibid., 243-246.
4. His Holiness the Dalai Lama, *The Essential Dalai Lama: His Important Teachings* (New York: Viking Penguin, 2005), 69.

Chapter 6
1. Doreen Virtue, *Chakra Clearing: Awakening Your Power to Know and Heal* (Carlsbad, CA: Hay House Inc., 1998), 81.
2. Virtue, *How to Hear Your Angels* (Carlsbad, CA: Hay House, Inc., 2007), chapters 5-8. Note that discussion of the "clairs" can be found in several of Doreen's books and is included in her Angel Therapy® trainings.

Chapter 8
1. Gregg Braden, *The Divine Matrix: Bridging Time, Space, Miracles, and Belief* (Carlsbad, CA: Hay House Inc., 2007), 32-35.

Chapter 10

1. Hicks, *Ask and It Is Given*. This is an excellent book. Also visit their Website: www.abraham-hicks.com for more information on their teachings.

Chapter 11

1. Michael Newton, *Journey of Souls: Case Studies of Life Between Lives* (Woodbury: Llewellyn Publications, 1996), 85-86.
2. Richard Bach, *Illusions: The Adventures of a Reluctant Messiah* (New York: Dell Publishing, 1997), 177.
3. Carroll, "The Eight Shifts of Enlightenment," fourth shift.

Chapter 12

1. Deepak Chopra, *The Seven Spiritual Laws of Success: A Practical Guide to the Fulfillment of Your Dreams* (San Rafael: Amber-Allen Publishing and New World Library, 1994), 67-68.
2. Chopra, *The Seven Spiritual Laws of Success*, 71-72.

Chapter 13

1. Tolle, *A New Earth*, 258.

Chapter 14

1. Elizabeth Gilbert, *Eat, Pray, Love: One Woman's Search for Everything Across Italy, India and Indonesia* (New York: Penguin Books, 2006), 327-328.

Chapter 15

1. Abraham Maslow, *Motivation and Personality* (New York: Harper, 1954), 91-93, 236.

2. Doreen Virtue (CD), *Chakra Clearing: A Morning and Evening Meditation to Awaken Your Spiritual Power* (Carlsbad, CA: Hay House, Inc., 1997).
3. Tachi-ren, *What Is Lightbody?*, 86-91.
4. Institute of HeartMath is located in Boulder Creek, CA. For research, education, and training information, visit: http://www.heartmath.org. For general information and to purchase materials, visit: http://www.heartmath.com.
5. Doc Childre and Deborah Rozman, *Transforming Stress: The Heartmath® Solution for Relieving Worry, Fatigue, and Tension* (Oakland: New Harbinger Publications, Inc., 2005), 31.
6. Childre and Rozman, *Transforming Stress*.

Chapter 16
1. Quan Yin, *The Pleiadian Workbook,* section two.

Chapter 17
1. Elizabeth Clare Prophet, *Violet Flame: To Heal Body, Mind & Soul* (Gardiner: Summit Publications, Inc., 1997), 31.
2. Doreen Virtue, *Chakra Healing: Awakening Your Spiritual Power to Know and Heal* (Carlsbad, CA: Hay House, Inc., 1998), 68-73.

Chapter 18
1. Campbell, *The Hero's Journey*, xv.

Suggested Reading

The following list is a sampler of some of the excellent books available to guide you as you continue your journey of spiritual transformation.

Cameron, Julia. *The Right to Write: An Invitation and Initiation into the Writing Life.* New York: Tarcher/Putnam, 1998. If you want to get excited about journaling, this book is for you. Author of *The Artist's Way.*

Childre, Doc, and Deborah Rozman. *Transforming Stress: The HeartMath® Solution for Relieving Worry, Fatigue, and Tension.* Oakland: New Harbinger Publications, Inc., 2005. One of many powerful HeartMath books available.

Choquette, Sonia. *Trust Your Vibes: Secret Tools for Six-Sensory Living.* Carlsbad, CA: Hay House, Inc., 2004. A helpful book on learning to follow your own guidance.

Gilbert, Elizabeth. *Eat, Pray, Love: One Woman's Search for Everything Across Italy, India and Indonesia.* New York: Penguin Books, 2006. An inspiring true story of spiritual awakening that will help you *want* to meditate regularly.

Hahn, Thich Nhat. *The Heart of Understanding.* Berkeley: Parallax Press, 1998. A fifty-four-page book that is regarded as the essence of Buddhist teaching.

Hay, Louise. *You Can Heal Your Life.* Carlsbad, CA: Hay House, Inc., 1999. Louise Hay is the guru of the mind-body-spirit connection.

Hicks, Esther and Jerry. *Ask and It Is Given: Learning to Manifest Your Desires.* Carlsbad, CA: Hay House, Inc., 2004. This book is the authority on working with the law of attraction.

Newton, Michael. *Journey of Souls: Case Studies of Life Between Lives*. Woodbury: Llewellyn Publications, 1994. A fascinating book. It will truly help you remember who you are.

Palmer, Helen. *The Enneagram: Understanding Yourself and the Others in Your Life*. San Francisco: Harper Collins, 1991. The title says it all. Studying this spiritually based personality system will provide you with an education in the nature of humanity.

Price, John Randolph. *The Abundance Book*. Carlsbad, CA: Hay House, Inc., 1996. This powerful minibook explains the law of attraction and provides a forty-day plan that will get you in the flow of your natural prosperity.

Quan Yin, Amorah. *The Pleiadian Workbook: Awakening your Divine Ka*. Santa Fe: Bear and Company, Inc., 1996. A heavy-duty ascension book packed with transformative energy work practices, meditations, etc.

Stubbs, Tony. *An Ascension Handbook: Channeled Material by Serapis*. Lithia Springs: New Leaf, 1999. A "how to" manual for ascending Lightworkers.

Tachi-ren, Tashira. *What Is Lightbody?* Lithia Springs: World Tree Press, 2005. A fairly intense little channeled ascension book that describes the process of increasing one's vibration, or lightbody. Very interesting.

Tamura, Michael J. *You Are the Answer: Discovering and Fulfilling Your Soul's Purpose*. Woodbury: Llewellyn, 2007. A wonderful book on spiritual awakening.

Tolle, Eckhart. *A New Earth: Awakening to Your Life's Purpose*. New York: Dutton, 2005. This book takes you from the dark woods of the ego into the timeless world of spirit. Author of *The Power of Now*.

Tribole, Evelyn, and Elyse Resch. *Intuitive Eating: A Revolutionary Program that Works.* New York: St. Martin's Griffin, 2003. The best book I've seen on dispelling the dieting myth and helping you love and honor your body.

Van Praagh, James. *Reaching to Heaven: A Spiritual Journey Through Life and Death.* New York: Dutton, 1999. This uplifting book will ease your fears of death as it helps you tune in to your soul. Author of *Talking to Heaven.*

Virtue, Doreen. *Chakra Clearing: Awakening Your Spiritual Power to Know and Heal.* Carlsbad, CA: Hay House, Inc., 1998. This is a great minibook containing meditations and visualizations to help you maintain healthy chakras. (Look for the companion meditation CD called *Chakra Clearing*).

Virtue, Doreen. *How to Hear Your Angels.* Carlsbad, CA: Hay House, Inc., 2007. A good introduction to the world of angels, with a focus on developing one's ability to receive divine guidance.

Virtue, Doreen. *The Lightworker's Way: Awakening Your Spiritual Power to Know and Heal.* Carlsbad, CA: Hay House, Inc., 1997. Doreen's personal story of spiritual awakening, as well as many valuable teachings.

Williamson, Marianne. *A Return to Love: Reflections on the Principles of A Course in Miracles.* New York: HarperPerennial, 1993. A clear and heartfelt interpretation of the life-changing teachings found in *A Course in Miracles.*

Wisehart, Susan. *Soul Visioning: Clear the Past. Create Your Future.* Woodbury: Llewellyn, 2008. This book will help you identify and follow the wisdom of your soul, while highlighting several leading-edge transformational practices.

About the Author

Jill Shinn holds a master's degree in transpersonal psychology. She is a licensed marriage and family therapist, a Reiki master, and an Angel Therapy Practitioner®. Jill teaches, speaks, and writes on various spiritual and psychological topics. She resides with her husband and two children in the San Francisco Bay Area.

Please visit her blog at: http://WakeUp-Sweetheart.blogspot.com

Please visit her Website at: www.WakeUpSweetheart.com

Made in the USA
San Bernardino, CA
19 April 2016